Meditations on the Character of God

Robin K. Schroeder

Front Cover Photo:
Multnomah Falls, Multnomah, Oregon
Taken while on trip with Japanese friends, 1998

Meditations on the Character of God

Copyright © 2003
Son-Risen Ministries
First Printing

ISBN: 0-9727658-0-8
Library of Congress Control Number: 2002096394

Printed in the USA by

MORRIS PUBLISHING

3212 East Highway 30 • Kearney, NE 68847 • 1-800-650-7888

Dedication

To:
Jesus Christ, my Lord and my God,
my parents, William & Dorothea Hulet
my husband, Jerry,
my children, Quinn, Darrin, Rebecca,
and Rachel,
and my grandchildren, Kendall, Kate,
Grant, and Alyssa

Acknowledgements

These devotionals were birthed out of a personal quest that ended up being shared with our church, Nara International Christian Center.

Years ago I heard a life-changing phrase, "We become like who we worship," followed by "Nearness brings likeness". These two statements changed my whole spiritual outlook. My personal desire was to really grasp the character of God. So as I worshipped Him, I would be changed to become more like Him.

I believe the more we grasp His character we will also be able to trust more, our faith will be strengthened and hope becomes solid, almost tangible with the power of the knowledge of God's eternal trustworthiness.

None of this writing would have been produced in any form without my husband, Jerry. His dedication to deciphering my scribbles, editing and pursuing all the details and technical aspects of all this have made this possible. His encouragement to keep writing—but keep it brief—have both frustrated me and inspired me. Frustrated because I want to be lengthy, I've had to content myself with lengthy thinking and abbreviated writing.

Thank you, Sheryl Park and Candie Ittner, for taking your valuable time to edit these daily devotionals into grammatically correct sentences, insuring that I didn't make any Biblical errors or stretch the rules of English too far.

Thanks also go to our wonderful church family who always are encouraging me to keep on writing...and to my mother, Dorothea Hulet, and sister, Phyllis Cryer, who are not just personal inspirations, but fantastic cheerleaders, and to my father, William A. Hulet, who went home to be with the Lord on August 9, 2000, whose greatest legacy was his encouragement to keep pursuing the Lord.

Robin K. Schroeder

Table of Contents

Our Creator God Who Enables	*1*
The Creator at Work in You	*8*
Characteristics of God's Love and Everlasting Commitment	*15*
God Loves You! You are Precious to Him!	*22*
The Challenge: Love As We Are Loved	*29*
Old Testament Lovingkindness Holds Hands With New Testament Grace, Part 1	*36*
Old Testament Lovingkindness Holds Hands With New Testament Grace, Part 2	*43*
Old Testament Lovingkindness Holds Hands With New Testament Grace, Part 3	*50*
Grace Expressed Is Mercy Experience, Part 1	*57*
Grace Expressed Is Mercy Experience, Part 2	*64*
Grace Expressed Is Mercy Experience, Part 3	*71*
Grace Expressed Is Mercy Experience, Part 4	*78*
Discovering God's Character in the Broad Places	*85*
The Lord Listens To & Shelters the Wounded Heart	*92*
God's Character of Righteousness	*99*
He Is All Our Righteousness	*106*
We Have a Living, Victorious Lord	*113*
Merciful Forgiveness, Marvelous Forgetfulness, Part 1	*120*
Merciful Forgiveness, Marvelous Forgetfulness, Part 2	*127*
The Blessings of God's DBL M-F Phenomenon	*134*
Faithfulness	*141*
Amazement at God's Glory	*148*
The Goodness of God	*155*
God's Goodness: A Promised Provision	*162*
God's Goodness Endures	*169*
The Key to Wisdom & Understanding	*176*
Holy is the Lord	*183*
Declarations of God's Holiness	*190*
Responses to God's Holiness	*197*

The Holy God Must Discipline ... 204

The Righteous Judge ... 211

Recognizing the Value of God's Judgments ... 218

In Praise of the Righteous Judge ... 225

What Does the Righteous Judge Do About Sin? ... 232

Jesus, Equal with Father God in Authority ... 239

Who Teaches Like Him (Job 36:22) ... 246

For He Instructs—In Right Judgment God Teaches (Isa.28:26) ... 253

The Teachable Heart ... 261

A Father To The Fatherless ... 268

Without Shadow of Turning ... 275

The Lord's Loving Sacrifice ... 282

Triumph In Christ ... 289

Secure In God's Everlasting Love ... 296

Letting Go & Letting God Be God ... 303

Like a Shepherd, the Lord Provides ... 310

Like a Shepherd, the Lord Guides to Green Pastures ... 317

The Lord Leads to Still Waters ... 324

Our Shepherd God Who Restores ... 331

Our Savior Shepherd ... 338

The Shepherd Who Protects & Sustains ... 345

Our Shepherd Reaches Out with Goodness and Mercy ... 352

Jesus, Pattern for Our Lifestyle ... 359

Our Creator God Who Enables

Isaiah 40:1-8

A new day and a New Year is here. But as in time past we can only live one moment at a time. Making the minutes count is what gives value to the hours, days, weeks, and years. Have you been going through trials and difficulties? Notice the first verse. "Comfort, yes, comfort My people!" says your God. *(NKJV)* Through all of the problems, the consequences of past choices, the disciplines we go through, there are certain, absolute truths we can count on 1) God is a God who comforts. 2) God sends people to show the way to come into relationship with Him. 3) He removes destruction so we can respond to Him. 4) God's glory and majesty will be revealed. 5) God's Word is absolute and eternal. We can count on His truth!

"Thank You, my Lord, for being a God who comforts. Thank You for Your judgments that reveal Your righteousness. And thank You for the teachers who show the way back to You! Thank You that Your Word stands eternal. You are a God who I can count on and I'm grateful!"

Isaiah 40:9-11

Our God is a God of victory. We can proclaim His truth unashamedly. In the Victor's presence are the rewards of experiencing His love, joy, and peace. His victory is shared with us. The Lord delights in caring for us, providing for us and guiding us as a Loving Shepherd would.

"Thank You, Lord, for Your majestic victory over all that would exalt itself over You. Thank You for Your loving care that surrounds, provides and guides. It is a wonder to me how You, the Sovereign God, love so completely, caring about every aspect of my life. It's sobering and humbling. Who am I that I should try to be in control? You, Lord, are the One whom I trust, for You are not just eternal, but gentle and loving, and You are my Shepherd."

Isaiah 40:12-20

God is greater than any force, any situation, or any problem. Do you have questions and fears about what the future holds? Why? Don't you know who holds the future? God's heavenly perspective can guide us through the maze of the present and the future.

"Thank You, Lord, for being greater than every challenge I face—every difficulty and every hurt. Thank You for Your grace that strengthens and holds me together. Thank You for Your loving character that surrounds me with so much care. What have I to fear when I have You?"

Isaiah 40:21-27

Our God is the Creator! When man still thought the earth was flat, God inspired Isaiah to write in verse 22 that "God sits above the circle of the earth...." Man's knowledge didn't hold—and never has held—a candle to our majestic, Creator God! And yet this all-powerful Creator God reaches out in love to each one of us. Humbling, isn't it?

"Thank You, Lord, for being there for me. When I consider Your majesty, Your greatness, and Your power, I realize that You want to use all of that in my life. But You have limited Yourself to my permission. I am humbled and awed! Lord, take full rein (and reign) over my life. I trust You with who I am and where I'm at."

Isaiah 40:21, 28
Romans 1:19-20
Psalm 19:1-4

L isten to God's Word with the realization of who God is. Did either of your parents ever say something like this? "I've told you and told you, but you didn't listen." Or those of you who are parents, have you not said the same thing? God is always reaching out and trying to get our attention so we will know the truth of who He is. What is your perception of God?

"Open my eyes, Lord, to the reality of who You are. Open my ears, Lord, to hear and comprehend Your truths as never before. Lord, I want this year to be a sincere quest in knowing You better and worshipping You wholeheartedly in everything I do and say."

Isaiah 40:28-29

Our God does not take naps or sleep. He is always there—even when we don't feel like He's there. He is not limited to our emotional feelings. He is in truth present and aware; we just need to, by faith, believe the truth of what we know. We won't ever know all that God does, but we can know the One who knows all. It sure takes the worry out of what we don't understand. Not being mechanically oriented, I don't understand how the oven works. But that doesn't mean that I don't use the oven...or don't trust it to do its job! Think about all the man-made things you use that you don't understand. But you expect them to work—cars, electricity, running water, TV, stereos, computers, can openers, electric knives, and on and on. Why do we trust transient, man-made things and not the all-powerful, all-knowing, loving Creator God?

"It is You, my Lord, whom I trust! Sometimes I forget how totally trustworthy and omnipotent You are! But the bottom line is that I trust You! You alone are worthy of my complete trust. Thank You for Your commitment to me. Lord, I want to respond to You with complete commitment and trust."

Isaiah 40:30-31
Ephesians 3:20

Our Creator God, who leads like a shepherd, is there for us in times of struggle. To those who wait on Him, delight in Him, seek Him first, He gives the ability to soar like an eagle, to overcome, discovering each time the creative ways God has to solve the otherwise unsolvable situations.

"Thank You, Lord, for Your creativity and the way You divinely empower us to overcome and be victorious in all of life's situations as we look to You in trust."

January 8

The Creator at Work in You

Hebrews 11:1-3

Do you ever feel inadequate? The situation seems desperate or purposeless. Good! Notice the end of verse 3. God created something out of nothing by His word alone! So look at yourself and your life and realize beyond a shadow of a doubt that by God's word your life can, and will be, put in order and you will be equipped for your intended purpose. The only ingredient you need is faith, which is the confidence in God that leads to committed obedience to His word demonstrated by your lifestyle.

"Depending on You, Lord, brings so many interesting situations to light. Walking by faith is never boring and is always an adventure! But if I can remember to keep my eyes on You and not on situations, then I can 'walk on water' (Matthew 14:25-32)."

8

2 Corinthians 5:17

When we believe in Christ we are made new. The things that controlled us before no longer have dominion over us. Sometimes it takes a while to learn this! Have you ever watched a child learning to walk? Hands are in the air holding on to Mom or Dad's fingers in the beginning. But even with the first steps, the hands are up like they still need to hold on. We'd look pretty silly as adults trying to walk like that! But we know we don't need to hold on to what controlled our steps in the beginning. Faith in Jesus makes us new creations! His work in our hearts continually creates newness and gives fresh starts. Our Creator knows how to make all things new!

"Thank You, Lord, for being the Creator who knows how to make me new! Even when I forget to walk by faith, You know how to remind me to trust and follow You unflinchingly."

2 Corinthians 5:17-21

We have been made new for a purpose. Our lives can be lived so we exemplify and teach the freeing truths of reconciliation with God. By our every word and action, our goal is to bring others to the joyous lifestyle of harmony with Him. We are ambassadors of this liberating truth. Jesus Christ, holy and perfect, took our sins on Him, paid the price for those sins, so that we might receive His righteousness. Why wouldn't we want to be ambassadors of the joyous truth of being made a new creation through Jesus?

"Thank You, Lord Jesus, for taking my sins to the cross and paying the price for what I have done. Thank You, Lord, that You won the victory over death and sin by Your resurrection. Lord, I am amazed at Your creative genius and humbled that You entrust believers to be Your ambassadors of truth. Everything You do reveals not just Your love, but also Your desire for relationship. It's awesome! Thanks!"

Ephesians 2:8-22

Because of being *re*-created in Christ Jesus by His grace when we accept Him as our Lord and Savior, we know experientially the truth of having access and nearness to God, our Father. We know the peace only Jesus can give. We can know true fellowship with other Christians as well.

But the best thing is to have the Spirit of God dwelling in our hearts. God created a way to purify our hearts so there is no darkness, emptiness, or sense of futility. Rather, we know true relationship and abiding peace.

"Lord, lead me today and each day on the paths that You have chosen so I might be Your ambassador of truth to others. I want them to recognize the joyous truths of knowing You!"

Romans 12:2
Ephesians 4:23-32

We are new creations by God's design through faith in Jesus. Our part is to receive this gift by faith. Then we are to put our faith into action by tuning out the things that would conform us to the unbelievers' ways and then tuning in to God's word so that our whole pattern of thinking and behaving is fresh and renewed. Some practical ways of doing this are: not letting anger have dominion over our thoughts and not allowing the devil, who is the deceiver, any foothold into our lives; being kind and helpful, compassionate and tenderhearted towards others; being forgiving just as God is, and clinging to God's creative grace that enables us to be all that He desires us to be.

"Lord, give me Your discernment so I can easily see the traps that the deceiver would use to tempt me away from Your ways. I pray that the 'words of my mouth and the meditations of my heart be acceptable to You, O Lord, my Strength and my Redeemer.' (Psalm 19:14)"

Philippians 1:6

He will continue to develop and perfect us and bring His plan to full completion. Isn't that wonderful? God's creative ways are fresh and new every day and individualized to each of our needs. Each creative way of God in our hearts gives us a new experience in Him. A new depth to His love and grace. A new reality of His character. What a joy to know Jesus!

Personalize Ephesians 3:14-21 and read it to the Lord.

Revelation 4:11, 5:12-13

All things were created by and through Jesus (Colossians 1:15-18). That means we—you and I—are physically and spiritually created! Worship Him by seeing afresh how worthy He is to be honored and respected. He is worthy of our praise and adoration. As we worship Him, our hearts open and we become more and more like Him. We are created for good works, yes. But growing closer to Jesus through worship brings the greatest transformation in our hearts and minds. **Nearness brings likeness**.

"Lord Jesus, You are worthy to receive praise, for You are the Lamb of God who paid the price to bring me into fellowship with the Father. Thank You for all you have done and all You continue to do in making me a new creation. You are amazing. Walking by faith with You is liberating and never dull! I honor You, my Lord and my God!"

Characteristics of God's Love and Everlasting Commitment

Galatians 3:29
James 2:23

Our God is creative and does not limit His expressions of love. As we read Old Testament promises to Israel, remember that those promises were given to Israel with full intent that they would be for all people who had faith like Abraham, the father of the Jewish nation. Faith in God creates a fertile field for friendship to grow. Love and friendship are intangible. Therefore, they are only received by faith.

"Thank You, Lord, for reaching out in love to me. Thank You for Your declarations of love by word and deed. Your love is incomprehensible in its scope and design. By faith I reach out to embrace it with all my heart and strength."

Jeremiah 31:3
Romans 8:38, 39

The Lord reaches out with everlasting love that is unstoppable. Think about this kind of commitment to love you and me. Are we worth this kind of unconditional, unstoppable love? No, not really! Except to God! The Lord knows our weaknesses and still has committed to love us with an everlasting love. How can we turn our backs on this kind of committed, unconditional love?

"Lord, I'm humbled and in awe of Your declarations of everlasting love. I know they're true because of all You do to show love. But I'm still amazed. Thank You, Lord. I want to cherish You with all my heart. But I find at times I fail. Yet I know Your love reaches to me even when I fail. Amazing! I love how You love me!"

Isaiah 53:4-6
Romans 5:8

God's actions declaring love were proclaimed by Isaiah. John 15:13 tells us the greatest love is expressed by laying down one's life for one's friends. Think about the fact that the love of God doesn't demand perfection from us before we can receive salvation. Rather, after salvation God's love is what changes us to be more like Him. The truth of God's love is expressed through the unselfish life, death, and resurrection of Jesus. By Jesus' death we receive the benefits of His taking our burdens and grief upon His shoulders. Because of our sinful thoughts and ways, Jesus was beaten and physically abused. For us to receive peace, Jesus paid the price. He was beaten so that we might receive healing. All of these benefits are ours even though mankind has rejected and dishonored Jesus. The eternal commitment of God's love is not conditional. It is steady and solid reaching through the ages to touch you and me.

"Thank You, Lord Jesus, for loving me just as I am. I stand amazed at Your supreme sacrifice for my benefit. You show me in every way that I am cherished. Lord, I don't want to be a spoiled brat, taking and demanding from You. Instead, I want to show You the honor and respect You deserve, as well as to love You wholeheartedly."

John 3:16-17

These are probably the most quoted verses in the Bible. But have you really looked at them? God's motivation for reaching out was His great love. God's love just keeps on giving. When we accept Jesus as our savior, God continues to express His love to us so our hearts can experience peace and serenity. God's great love reaches out through all history for hearts willing to accept, respond and honor His great gift.

"Thank You, Lord, for Your wonderful plan of salvation. Thank You that Your love stretches and reaches out to me and finds creative ways to surround me with Your love."

Deuteronomy 7:9

(A promise for us because of the father of faith, Abraham.)

To accept the eternal commitment of God's unconditional love, we must recognize the fact of God's love. If we recognize that the love of God is true, then we must understand that the truth of God's love is not only for mankind in general, but also personally directed to each individual. Although we love our family as a whole, we also love each person as an individual.

In addition, we must then know that God's steadfast love is a commitment and will not be withdrawn. Sovereign God has made Himself vulnerable to us by reaching out in pure love and giving us the choice to respond to Him.

"Thank You, Lord, for being open and vulnerable with Your unconditional, steadfast love. I'm grateful not to be a puppet that is forced to act. But I am a person who chooses to respond. Lord, I know beyond a shadow of a doubt the truth of Your love. I know I can trust all my tomorrows into Your loving hands."

1 John 3:1-2

The incredible quality of God's love reaches throughout history and around the world to draw people into His family. It's amazing! It's a wonder! It's a comfort! Many people who have rejected God's love have also rejected the true followers of the Lord. As those who are rejected for being Christians, all we can do is love those who reject us with God's love. Being rejected and despised by man didn't stop Jesus from loving mankind and giving His life for us all. Now, because we have received God's love, we must pass it on to others. We have no fear for the future because we can trust God and know that circumstances work for good to those who love and trust God.

"Thank You, Lord, for the comfort of Your love and the confidence Your love gives. You are great and wonderful. Your love is amazing and comforting. Lord, I choose daily to respond to Your love and to let Your love flow freely from me to others—even to those who despise me because I am a Christian. Let Your love flow through me as an example of who You are."

Ephesians 1:4
Psalm 139

All things were created by and through Jesus (Colossians 1:15-18). That means God's love began before the earth was created. He knows you and everything about you. After all, the creative God, the Maker of the universe, designed you uniquely to receive His gift of love. Then because of that great love, He left the choice of receiving Him up to you. How have you chosen to respond to His love?

"Lord, You created me and know me and yet You still love me. Thank You. I choose to respond to Your love fearlessly. Other's opinions don't matter in the light of who You are. You are more important to me than any person. Your love has amazed me and is the greatest experience of my life. Thank You!"

God Loves You!
You are Precious to Him!
Zephaniah 3:17

Love is not tangible; we can't touch it. We know love by experience. Love is multi-dimensional; therefore it is known through a variety of experiences. Look at the multiple expressions of God's love in this verse—Immanuel, God is with us, the Mighty One, our Savior. He rejoices over us with great joy and gladness. His love will be our source of quiet confidence. He will rejoice over you with singing. This last phrase has a special meaning to me because my dad always rocked and sang made-up songs about his kids and grandkids, telling them how wonderful and special each one is. So I can imagine Father God gathering His beloved child in His arms and singing songs of joy.

"Thank You, Lord, for not just being the Mighty One, Savior, majestic Lord of lords, but also for rejoicing and singing songs of joy over me. That expresses so much about Your love…knowing as a child, I'm not just a duty, but also a joy. Thanks for Your amazing love."

Isaiah 43:1-7
2 Corinthians 5:7

God knows us and calls us by name. He has redeemed us and cares for us. We have no cause to fear. Even when circumstances overwhelm, God's love is so pure and complete that we are surrounded and protected.

Why? Because each one of us is precious in His sight. Have you seen the face of a new mom or dad looking at their newborn? The love, amazement, and joy on their faces is evident. That baby is their beloved, precious child, and the love they feel overwhelms them. God's love for us is immeasurably more pure than that and He delights in us!

"It's amazing to me that You, the Holy God, find me precious! Your love is awesome, Lord! Knowing Your love experientially is the greatest treasure and source of hope. You are incredible, my Lord. Thank You for Your unfailing love!"

2 Thessalonians 2:16-17

God's love—past, present, and future—is the bulwark upon which we can rest. God loves and gives. Have you ever tried to love without giving? It's impossible. When you love someone, you delight in giving service as well as things to that person. God loves us, and among the ways He expresses that love is through continually encouraging and giving hope to comfort and strengthen us. He enables us to be steadfast. God's love is perfect and pure.

"Thank You, Lord Jesus, for establishing my steps by Your love. Thank You for Your comfort and the hope I have in You. Your expressions of love are a delight to me."

John 10:11-18
John 15:13

Jesus' love was so great that He willingly laid down His life. He took our sins and died a gruesome death on the cross to pay the price for our sins so we could receive His righteousness by the power of His resurrection. No greater love has ever been expressed than what Jesus did for you and me. Men didn't kill Jesus even though it was for mankind's sin that Jesus died. Jesus laid down His life. Remember that; cherish that; think about it and let it permeate your thoughts. Every time you do, think, or say something that is less than kind or selfish, remember that was the reason Jesus willingly laid down His life to pay the price for even that sin.

"Thank You, Jesus, for paying the price for my sin. Thank You for giving me Your righteousness in exchange for my sins! Thank You for Your resurrection power that enables me to be more than a conqueror. You are wonderful!"

Proverbs 3:11-12, 9:8-9, 12:1

L ove can be expressed by giving correction. Would you stop your child from playing with fire, running in the busy street, drinking bleach? Of course! If the child persisted, what would you do to change their behavior?

Our second son had uncanny and often creative ways of discovering dangerous things to do. He, more than the other three, needed extra supervision and extra discipline, correction, and direction. He had no fear of danger and, therefore, had to be trained to avoid things like jumping off the roof of the house, riding his bike (still with training wheels) down a steep hill into oncoming traffic, sticking keys into electric sockets, etc. Was he loved less because he was in a constant state of discipline (or so it seemed)? No! Love dictates safe boundaries. What is your response to God's correction?

"Thank You, Lord, for loving me enough to correct me. I want to respond wisely to Your instruction and to be teachable. Thank You for not enabling my weaknesses, but rather teaching and training me to overcome, and supplying me with Your resurrection power and redeeming grace."

Hebrews 12:5-13

God doesn't correct in anger, but with love. Loving discipline brings repentance and righteousness and is for our own benefit. Learning to live a life that honors God means we need to be trained to think and respond in godly ways. Therefore, the old ways have to be untaught. Hebrews 5:8 tells us that even though Jesus was God's Son, He learned obedience by the things which He suffered.

Are you going through a time when you feel overwhelmed? What is God teaching you? How do you look for ways to praise instead of complain? How do you find ways of expressing love instead of anger? How do you stop looking for someone to blame, but rather accept the responsibility yourself? Think about it! In what way is God instructing you for your own good?

"Lord, open my eyes to understand Your correction so I will respond correctly. Even when frustrated by my circumstances, I don't want to rebel against You. Help me to respond to Your instruction with a heart of wisdom."

Psalm 103

God's love is expressed by His forgiveness, and by His healing of our body, soul, and mind. He redeems us and overwhelms us with grace, love and mercy. Of course, a relationship like this satisfies! Don't you just love the fact that God removes our sins from us as far as the east is from the west? God's mercy and love deserve our praise. He alone is worthy of worship!

As a parent, one of the greatest things our children have said (especially our second "always-in-trouble" son) is, "Thanks. I'm so grateful for your training." If we as humans feel that, how much more deserving God is of our gratitude! Let's bless Him with our praise, worship and gratitude.

"Thank You, Lord, for Your loving teaching, training, and instruction. Your graciousness and mercy are overwhelmingly abundant! I'm so grateful for all the ways You reach out to me in love. You comfort me while training me and then enable me to overcome wrong attitudes, thoughts, patterns, and reactions. And You do it for my own good! Thank You for Your perfect love!"

The Challenge: Love As We Are Loved

John 15:9-14
Romans 12:1-2

Challenge: Love as we are loved. How easy is it to get wrapped up in our own personal feelings of hurt or anger, or feelings of betrayal and disappointment? *But*, those feelings must be our sacrifice to God. Those feelings, when harbored, become a shield and a defense against vulnerability and loving unconditionally. Our pattern and example is Jesus who understands all of our feelings because He experienced the same situations. Yet He still unconditionally loves us without reservation!

"Lord Jesus, thank You for loving me completely and unconditionally. Thank You for cherishing me and showing me the significance You place on me by giving Your life for me. The victory of resurrection is what I need to empower me to give up the feelings that war with the desire to love as You do. Teach me Your ways, show me Your paths, my Lord and my God."

Philippians 2:1-11
Matthew 5:38-48

Self-centered, selfish motives have no place in loving like Jesus does. Turning the other cheek—doesn't that mean to drop your defenses and be vulnerable, even to pain? How can we do this? Doesn't Jesus exemplify this? We must put our hurts to death on the altar of sacrifice. Before Jesus came, sacrifices had to be perfect to illustrate the perfect Lamb of God, Jesus. But since that once-and-only Perfect Sacrifice was given, the sacrifices we give are personal, ugly, imperfect, self-centered things! It is too easy to make friends with wrong emotions and reactions that would war against being like Christ Jesus.

"Lord, show me those selfish, destructive thought patterns that would destroy Christ-likeness in me. Enable me to drop the shields I erect against others. For You and You alone are my Shield and my Protector. I choose to trust You, and not my limited perceptions. Take my hand, Lord, and lead me in Your ways."

1 John 4:2-21

No fear in love (v 18). So we turn the other cheek, go the second mile and still the person betrays our trust and rejects us. Yet we are to love. 1 Corinthians 13:4-7 tells us that love doesn't keep track of offenses. Psalm 103:12 tells us that as far as the east is from the west God separates us from our sins. God's love values the person, but He never condones sin. He hates the sin but loves the person. I can remember being angry because one of our children had done something very self-destructive. I cried and told him, "I'm so angry because you hurt my child." My love for him was great, but I hated what he had done because of the pain inflicted on himself. If I, an imperfect human, can feel that way, how much more God hates the way sin destroys the ones He loves. If we can see others through God's eyes of love, we will be able to separate the person from the action and love—truly love—them.

"Lord, You've told us that perfect love casts out fear. Let Your perfect love flow through me, taking away my fears of being vulnerable to hurt and rejection. Lord, let me see the people You've brought into my life with Your eyes of love, forgiveness and discernment. I can't do it apart from Your enabling."

Luke 6:27-38

Does anyone else get hung up on the phrase, "Do good to those who hate you…"? Acting nobly toward those who hate you…even blessing them? Ouch! That's hard. "But God demonstrated His own love for us in that while we were yet sinners Christ died for us." (Romans 5:8) Give love to others wholly and unconditionally and discover the joy of the Lord healing your heart, filling you with His love, peace, and joy.

People are not our source of complete, healing love. God is! Forgiving others keeps our focus on the love of the Lord at work in our hearts, to heal and make us whole and complete.

"Lord, it feels like the things that happen to me by other's hateful actions are what dictate my heart's responses. Yet, Lord, I know the truth is Your love is all I need to fill every painful cavity in my heart. Your grace will enable me to reach out in confidence and repay meanness and contempt with love and kindness. I need You, Lord, for I cannot do it without Your enabling grace and resurrection power."

Romans 12:21,13:10
2 Timothy 1:7

Love doesn't hurt others. Love will overcome evil, for God has not given us a spirit of fear, but of power and of love and of a sound mind. Isn't the secret then to learn how to become functional in the well-balanced calm and disciplined mind that is our gift from God? He gives His grace, fully and adequately, so we might experience the fullness and wholeness of mind He wants to give us. The limitations are self-inflicted and are not from the Lord. His desire to see us whole, and His generous grace and love are there for us to learn how to receive and live by His resurrection power.

"Lord, I want all that You have for me to enable me to live my life as a testimony to Your love and grace. Open my eyes and heart to receive. Fill me, Lord, with Your grace and love."

1 John 3:16-24

God doesn't ask of us more than He gives. He doesn't even ask of us more than He can enable us to do. It's up to us to decide daily to receive, in order to live a life that honors God and is a lighthouse to others, exhibiting the truth of God's love. Jesus is the pattern we must choose to follow. Are you willing to offer personal hurts and perceived abuses to Him who wants to heal and be your place of security?

"Lord, You are my hiding place! You are my rock of security. Take my hurts and frustrations. Fill me with Your love, joy, and peace. Enable me to be a lighthouse to shine the truth of Your love and grace. I rest in You."

Galatians 2:20-21, 5:22-25

We are instructed to be dead to destructive emotions, self-centered motivations, and all those things that would keep us from a close relationship with God. We are to willingly crucify them so we might know experientially the wholeness only His love and grace can bring.

The result of crucifying those things is the growth of the fruit of the Spirit in our lives. What do others see in your life? Does your life shine with God's love?

"Lord, shine through me! I recognize that I am the one who limits Your power, grace and love. Lord, I drop my shields and open my heart to You. I choose to put to death those destructive emotions that keep me from receiving and giving Your love and grace. I trust You with my life, my Lord and my God."

Old Testament Lovingkindness Holds Hands With New Testament Grace, Part 1

Psalm 17:5-8

Sometimes it is easy to take God's loving-kindness for granted. This is both good and bad. If taking grace for granted means a complete and expectant confidence in God that you are resting in, that's good! But if it means abusing His grace to do your own thing just because you know He'll be forgiving, then you've missed the point of God's loving-kindness. Don't forget that He is also the righteous Judge! *Rest in His grace* as a loyal and faithful child, but *don't abuse it*!

"Lord, I realize that the more I respond in faithfulness and loyalty to You, the more I will experience close relationship with You and the more I will experience the depth of Your grace. Open my eyes to the various ways You shower my life with Your lovingkindness."

John 1:14-18

The Savior came and through His life, death, and resurrection, we can realize the magnitude of God's grace and truth. I try to write of the truth of godly principles. But in writing of God's character, especially His grace, it touches so many personal experiences that I am compelled to express "the truth of the service station."

When my brother was four or five years old, he would use that phrase in his "sermons" when he'd pretend to be a preacher. (Incidentally, he later did become a preacher.) To me the phrase means, "A truth that gives you GO POWER!"

"Lord, teach me the truth of Your grace that gives power. I want to live a life pleasing to You!"

John 1:14-18

Note verse 16, "And of His fullness we have all received...." Are you walking in that fullness? Are you laboring, feeling heavy and overwhelmed by burdens? Perhaps you are trying to operate in a "Fred Flintstone" car, self-pedaled instead of powered by God's high-octane grace!

"Lord, open my eyes to the areas of my life that are self-propelled so I may surrender them to Your grace. I want to be the apple of Your eye, hidden in the shadow of Your wings and fully operational by Your high-octane grace!"

Psalm 15:1-15

One of God's greatest blessings to me was a mother who not only taught me godly principles, but also used every opportunity to reinforce the truth of them in everyday life.

David's heritage also included women of faith such as Ruth and Rahab. They left everything familiar because they knew the truth of who God is. Knowing Him was the most important thing in their lives. What a rich heritage!

Your experiences of living and exemplifying godly truth and principles and the obvious blessings of God's grace that you reap will touch and teach many lives. The more you experience the Lord in relationship, the more your life will touch and make a difference in others' lives.

"Lord, the cry of my life is to know You more. I'm greedy with desire. I know that is the only greed that blesses not just me, but will also touch my children and grandchildren. Lord, I want to be a light on the hillside displaying the wonder of Your grace and love!"

Romans 5:2, 15, 17, 20-21

L ook at how grace is described in each of these verses. God's grace is greater and more abundant than any sin or abuses of the past. Nothing we have done or have experienced in the past or present, or will do in the future, can be as great as God's lovingkindness expressed by His remarkable grace.

"Lord, I know your grace is more abundant, more powerful and full of strength than anything I face or experience. The problem is my forgetting that Your grace is abundantly available! Open my eyes, my memory, and my understanding daily to the reality of Your grace."

Romans 5:2, 15, 17, 20-21

Grace gives us the freedom to stand and to walk. Have you ever had an injury that prevented you from walking? I have.

I had taken the simple act of walking for granted until I literally couldn't stand. I no longer take walking for granted. It's now a joy! Oh, that we would relish and enjoy the privilege of being immersed in, strengthened by, and freed by God's abundant grace!

"Thank You for knowing my weaknesses, and yet still faithfully providing Your grace to enable me to do what You've called me to do. You are so good to me!"

Psalm 36:5-11

Under the shadow of Your wings…. That place is in the presence of God pictured in the Old Testament on the top of the Ark of the Covenant that was called the Mercy Seat. This symbolized atonement (the harmonious relationship provided by God), covenant (loyal promise) and provision.

"Lord, Your loyalty amazes me. Your desire for a close, harmonious relationship overwhelms me. Your constant provision humbles me. You are in every way an awesome God! I am grateful!"

Old Testament Lovingkindness Holds Hands With New Testament Grace, Part 2

John 10:18
1 Corinthians 11:23-26
Isaiah 53:4-6

The greatest gift of love is ours! Jesus willingly laid down His life. It wasn't comfortable either. Not only did He pay the price for our sins, but He did it by allowing Himself to be vulnerable to betrayal, denial, and rejection. Why? Because His love and the love of the Father reached out, not with chocolate or flowers, but with flesh that was beaten to a bloody pulp. The Son of God died on a crude, splintery cross to say, "I love you! I willingly paid the price to give you abundant life!" The joy of resurrection liberates us from the power of sin. But never forget the great cost that was paid because of His love for you!

"Thank You, my Lord and my God! There is none like You! You are worthy of all praise and honor. Thank You for Your every expression of love. I'm humbled by Your great love!"

Psalm 36:5-11

Have you ever watched a very young child trying to put on clothes and shoes? Two legs in one pant leg, shirt on backward, or shoes on the wrong feet. Yet when you try to help, they cry out, "I want to do it myself!" They need help but their stubborn pride keeps them from receiving it. The ark was covered in gold to symbolize God's throne and rulership as the Sovereign Lord. What is the reality of your relationship with the Lord? Are you nestled in that place of blessing under the shadow of His wings, recognizing Him as your source as well as your Lord? Or are you being tripped up by your stubborn pride?

"Lord, Your lovingkindness and grace are precious to me. Open my eyes to see where my pride demands to do my own thing—and I fall flat on my face. I'd rather enjoy the abundance of blessing that comes from being in right relationship with you."

2 Corinthians 5:17-21

Christ has done everything necessary to give us spiritual freedom. We need to remember to be grateful and not abuse His grace. What causes us to abuse His grace?

"Lord, show me areas of my life where I abuse Your grace."

2 Corinthians 5:17-21

Two main causes of abusing God's grace are pride and shame. When I was about eight, I remember trying to cover up my disobedience by dressing in good clothes and acting responsibly by eating my peas at dinner (peas...yuck!). But, a dirty tomboy dressed up in pink, eating peas, is both a pathetic picture and a wretched experience. My wise mother saw through my "disguise." Shame and pride get us into awkward situations. Why not stop doing the things that take God's grace in vain and start experiencing the fullness of His grace!

"Lord, my desire is to be an ambassador of Your grace and not a foolish example of pride and shame. Teach me to tune my ears into Your voice so that each day will be rich in the enjoyment of Your grace."

Psalm 42

What do you do when depression threatens to drown you with discouragement and helplessness? When all you can remember are the "good ol' days"? Depression puts blinders over our eyes to prevent a clear view of God's grace. This is the very time we must remember to *hope in God.* The Lord *commands* His lovingkindness to us. It is there for us to experience and depend on. Let's not waste it by not using it!

"Thanks, Lord, for always being there. Lift anything that works in my mind to keep or distract me from seeing the reality of Your grace. Thank You for being my Enabler."

Psalm 42

Here in Japan there are an abundance of hot springs, both natural and man-made. One place we have gone to has a waterfall to sit under and it beats the pain out of your shoulders and neck. Then you can sit in a Jacuzzi and let the bubbles melt away your muscular stress. It's wonderful! Do you realize that we have the spiritual equivalent? "God's Grace Hot Springs" overflow with strength to melt away mental and emotional stress and bless you out of your socks!

"Lord, why don't I remember the free access I have to Your 'Grace Hot Springs?' I am blessed because of Your gracious loving-kindness. You are worthy of all praise and glory, I'm grateful to be Your child!"

Psalm 92

Declaring God's loving-kindness in the morning is a declaration of the faith and the hope we have in Him. The evening is when we can tell the ways His faithfulness was expressed. Remember that God's faithfulness is what strengthens our hope and faith and gives us the confidence to face each new day and each new challenge.

"Thank You, Lord, for all that You are and for all that You've been and for the hope I have for all my tomorrows because of You."

Old Testament Lovingkindness Holds Hands With New Testament Grace, Part 3

2 Corinthians 12:9-10

God's grace is sufficient How true! What is your weakest area? Rejoice! When given to God it becomes your greatest strength. Character strength can be our greatest weakness because we don't see our need for God, which means it's a weakness. Funny how that works, isn't it?

"It's good to know, Lord, that Your grace, like Your love, is immeasurable. Thank You for Your loving-kindness that strengthens me."

2 Corinthians 12:9-10

How about applying God's grace to situations that leave us feeling alone or lost or isolated? It's very hard for me to be away from our 2 and "½" grandchildren. Their pictures—even the "½" grandson's sonograms—are plastered all over the kitchen. There are pictures in every room and a heart that longs to hold the other two grandchildren. But God shows the reality of His grace by filling my heart with joy and peace. More than that, He gives me spiritual promises to pray for them. What is not there physically is made up for in many ways: spiritually holding them in the arms of prayer, having other little ones to shower God's love on, and God's deep-down comfort that words can't express. Yes, God's grace is more than sufficient! Difficulties are the opportunities to dig deep into His abundant grace!

"Thank You, my precious Lord, for Your grace is abundant and comforting. I'm so grateful! Bless Your holy name."

Psalm 103:1-14

The Lord blesses us, beautifies us, and gives us dignity with His lovingkindness and tender mercies. He satisfies! Why do we humans embrace emotions that distract us from God's grace: self-pity, living in the past or in the future, pride, selfishness, depression, discouragement, anger, unforgiveness? What is keeping you from the full expression of God's gracious lovingkindness?

"Show me, Lord, the things that preoccupy my mind and blind me to all of the wonderful blessings You want to shower me with. Thank You for Your patience. You are wise and good. I'm glad I can trust You with me."

Psalm 103:1-14

When I was 17 years old, my brother died. At that time, I saw the beauty, dignity, and grace God pours into lives surrendered to Him. There was enough money for only two tickets to the U.S., and my dad couldn't leave me alone in Tokyo to deal with the death of my brother. So he graciously and willingly sacrificed the closure he needed so that I could go. My mom and my sister-in-law also exhibited glorious and abundant grace, and my life was touched, challenged, and inspired by their responses. God's amazing tenderness is expressed graciously at all times, and is especially bountiful in times of pain.

"Thank You, Lord, for the grace I have experienced and for Your lovingkindness and tender mercies I've observed in others. You are so good! Show me ways to "be Jesus" to others as so many have been to me."

Ephesians 2:4-10

Grace is multi-faceted and deep. Grace reaches out to us while we are still sinners to draw us into the family of God through salvation provided by Jesus. Grace gives us heavenly perspective. His grace is for the past, present, and future.

"Lord, You are so wonderful. Your grace knows no end. I love the creative ways You find to express Your love and make Your grace available."

Ephesians 2:4-10

You can't stop the flow from God. But you can choose not to use it. That's like sitting in the car refusing to use the key, complaining and wondering why you aren't going anyplace. Don't waste God's grace. It's free and He wants us to avail ourselves of it. Stop worrying about the unknown and dive into His grace. Discover the wonder of His ability to take care of you in *all* circumstances! If you had a choice between a Rolls Royce and a wrecked vehicle that didn't run, which would you choose? God's grace is the Rolls. Our stubbornness is the broken-down vehicle.

"Thank You for Your patience with me. I mean to take the "Rolls" but sometimes I forget. I try to drive the broken-down wreck of my own way. It's foolish, I know. Lord, You're good! And Your patience is amazing."

Isaiah 63:7-9

Tell people how good God is. We have a great treasure. However, the more you share this treasure with others, the more you learn about it. It is eternal. Look for ways to express His grace in your life and be blessed by remembering and by sharing. Build your own, and others', faith by passing along expressions of God's goodness toward you.

"Lord, send people who will have hearing hearts and give me words to express the wonder of Your grace. Build others' faith and my own as Your grace is declared. You are a wonder and so very precious. Thank You for being You!"

Grace Expressed Is Mercy Experienced, Part 1

Colossians 3:12-17

This wonderful, loving, forgiving, and comforting grace needs to be expressed in more ways than with words only. By our actions toward others and in our praise to the Lord, we can show God our gratitude. When we respond to others lovingly, we put His grace into action and God is blessed. When we respond with the "love words" of praise, He is blessed.

Let Jesus be seen in you in word and deed!

"Lord, may I honor You in word and deed. Show me how and enable me so that my life will be an expression of Your grace."

Genesis 39:20-23

Mercy is strongest in the midst of difficulties. Joseph was unjustly accused and thrown into prison. He had a choice to whine and yell at God for the injustice or to flourish amidst seemingly hopeless circumstances. What about your situation? How are you responding?

"Lord, I need You every hour! I need Your guidance and instruction to rightly respond to difficulties. Open my eyes to see the challenge of faith so I will be able to experience Your mercy and blessings."

Genesis 39:20-23

This situation would seem depressing and hopeless at best, "but the Lord was with Joseph and showed him mercy and loving-kindness and gave him favor in the eyes of the warden of the prison." *(Amplified)* Joseph's imprisonment was the tool God used to elevate Joseph to second-only-to-Pharaoh in Egypt. Difficulties, no matter how hopeless they seem to be, are God's stage to show mercy and bring out greatness.

"Lord, I need to comprehend the truth that you are with me in the midst of all situations. I desire to respond in a way that honors and glorifies You. Teach me how, my Lord."

Exodus 15:1-18

These verses are a wonderful expression of praise recognizing the things God did and recognizing His character of holiness, mercy, etc.

"Lord, I want to praise You more with my whole heart in word, song and artistic expression, as well as in deed. Please show me how!"

Exodus 14:10-12

The same ones who had been praising became complaining, fearful, and faithless people. God didn't change. His mercy continued to reach out to them. What about you? Do you whine and complain, and become discouraged at obstacles? Or are you like Joseph, who faced his seemingly hopeless situation without complaint, believing God and trusting Him to make a way? Do you have 20/20 hindsight, or are you a person of vision, seeing God at work even in the dark times?

"Lord, open my eyes to see the victory You have for me in the midst of the struggles. I want to be seated with You in heavenly places maintaining a godly perspective. My desire, Lord, is to live a life of victory, seeing not the difficulties, but Your mercy and grace in the middle of it all."

Numbers 14:17-19
Micah 6:8

Again the Israelites were caught ranting and raging against God. Regrettably, negative thoughts, expressions, and complaining are contagious.

However, God used the negativity of the Israelites to provoke Moses to intercede for the people. How do you respond to others' negative words and behavior?

"Lord, help me to understand that negative experiences become positive when I turn to You. You created this way of giving beauty for ashes."

Numbers 14:17-19
Micah 6:8

This negative experience of the Israelites became a positive experience for Moses. By interceding for the people, Moses developed a patient, merciful, and humble spirit that also recognized justice. What is the character of the people who surround you? What kind of response does God want from you?

"Lord, it is easy to judge and condemn others, forgetting Your desire for me to be just, merciful, and humble. Lord, open my eyes to see others as You do and to intercede in prayer rather than to be negative and critical. Thank You for Your mercy when I have failed to recognize Your call to intercession. Fill me with Your wisdom. It is pure, peaceable, gentle, yielded, full of mercy, and without partiality or hypocrisy. Bless You, Lord, for Your generous mercy to me!"

Grace Expressed Is Mercy Experienced, Part 2

Deuteronomy 10:12-13

Deuteronomy (fifth book of the Bible) contains Moses' farewell to the Israelites. In it he reminds the generation of people who God is to them and the value of obedience to God's word. Exodus 3:41 says that God talked face to face with Moses. That does indicate that Moses knew God's character pretty well!

"Lord, I know You are a friend who is closer than a brother and that You delight in revealing Your character and in teaching godly principles. Open my heart to understand so that I will grow closer to You."

Deuteronomy 10:12-13

Throughout Deuteronomy we can see how much Moses respected the Lord his God. The questions we must ask ourselves: "How am I responding to God's love, grace, and mercy?" "Can I adequately express to others the truth of who God is to me?"

"As You are teaching me, Lord, of Your character, showing me how to grow closer to You, please give me understanding on how to whet others' appetites to know You as well."

Deuteronomy 6:4-5

What does it mean to love with all your heart, mind and strength? The heart refers to our innermost self—that part of us that makes up our character and personality—the secret place inside which feels, thinks, and decides. Our mind is where we think, reason, and receive understanding. It is vital that all we are is responding to God. After all, God loves us with all His heart and mind. We are God's top priority. Shouldn't He be ours?

"Thank You for Your committed love to me! You are my Lord and my God! More than that, You are a true Friend, Father, and Shepherd. You are always there for me. I want to be faithful to and steadfast towards You. But Lord, often I fail. Show me how to make my desire for steadfastness a reality."

Deuteronomy 7:6-11

Deuteronomy is filled with the promises of blessing when we live a life that honors God. It also tells us the consequences for disobedience and living a self-centered life that doesn't honor God.

"Lord, the phenomenon of obedience is experiencing a wonderful relationship with You, as well as receiving abundant blessings. Engrave this truth in my heart to enable me to always remember these truths."

Deuteronomy 7:6-11

We need to know in our hearts, minds, and spirits that the Lord our God *IS* God.

And what kind of God is He? Faithful and merciful. He keeps His covenant and He gives mercy to those who love Him. We obey God because of our love, respect, and honor towards Him.

"Enable me, Lord, to keep in mind the truth of the blessings of obedience when I'm faced with decisions of whether to honor You or whether to behave in a self-centered way.
Thanks!"

Deuteronomy 7:6-11

It is when living a life committed to Him, not compromising godly standards and principles, that each one of us truly discovers the depth of His love, mercy, and grace. Think about the aspects of the enduring relationships you have. Faithfulness, commitment, respect, trustworthiness, and mutual enjoyment of each other are just some of the necessary ingredients. Shouldn't our relationships be characterized by these same attributes? Doesn't He deserve the best we have in response to His great love?

"Lord, You alone are worthy of honor and glory. I don't want any compromises in my responses to You! Lord, it is You and You alone that I worship. I want my life to honor You in all that I say and do."

Deuteronomy 30:19-20

A key word here is "choose". God gives us a choice to worship and serve Him. He didn't create us to be puppets, but made Himself vulnerable by giving humans the free will to accept or reject Him. What a remarkable freedom God has given us. He warns of the consequences of wrong choices and tells of blessings of wise choices so we will choose correctly. What is your choice?

"Lord, thank You for giving me the freedom to choose. I know that wisdom comes from You, so I choose to worship You and gain more of your wisdom in making right choices."

Grace Expressed Is Mercy Experienced, Part 3

Isaiah 1:1-20

"Wishy-washy" best describes the Israelites' relationship with God. They were, as a nation, not committed to following God. Amazingly, every time they turned to God, He was merciful and rescued them. When their self-centered choices caused them to spiral down to desperate situations, they would, as their last resort, call on God.

What about you? Do you cruise along sowing self-indulgences until you've reaped their consequences? Do you turn to God only when you are desperate?

"Lord, help me to grasp that negative experiences become positive when I turn to You. You have a way of giving beauty for ashes."

2 Chronicles 17:3-6

King Jehoshaphat delighted in honoring and worshipping the Lord. Under his leadership the people turned to God. The king discovered the pleasure and joy in loving the Lord with all his heart, soul and might. His life was a light pointing to God in the midst of a dark history of national rebellion.

Where do you find delight? Have you immersed yourself in God's grace so that it is a daily reality? Is your response to God from your heart and mind or is it only based on outside difficulties?

"Lord, when all is said and done, I hope it can be said about me that I delighted in honoring and worshipping You. May my life always be an arrow pointing to You!"

2 Chronicles 20:1-13
1 Peter 5:5-9

King Jehoshaphat determinedly sought the Lord. He proclaimed a fast so everyone's focus would be on humbling themselves before the Lord. In Jehoshaphat's prayer (vs. 3-12) he recognized who God was, what He had done, and the hope He was for the nation's future. Then they waited to hear from God.

"Lord, humbling myself to You is the only way to make You the Lord of my life in fact and in deed. It's exciting to realize that only full surrender to You brings complete and overwhelming victory! It's amazing to experience Your ways!"

73

2 Chronicles 20:14-17

Often we try fighting spiritual battles we simply aren't equipped to handle. We need to recognize that they are God's battles and stop trying to do things in our own strength or reasoning. We need to position ourselves to be where God wants us physically as well as spiritually, stand firm, trust God, and see the mighty hand of God!

"Thank You for not just being my defense, but also for taking the offense. Where You lead, I will follow because You are the Victor always!"

2 Chronicles 20:19-19

King Jehoshaphat's response to God's word and direction was to worship and praise Him—all before the battle was visibly won. Seek God, release your mental tug-of-war, and respond to His direction in worship and praise. Then you will experience a freedom of spirit you've never known before.

"Thank You, Lord, not just for giving the victory, but also for the mental and emotional release worship and praise brings. You are more than wonderful. You are not just the Almighty God; You are also my Daddy! That's totally, awesomely cool."

2 Chronicles 20:20

"Believe in the Lord your God and you shall be established." It's the same today. Why debate and wonder what will happen if you, by faith, believe and trust God? Let God be God! The battle we worry about is His! Believe, trust, and your way will be established.

"Praise You, Lord, for Your mercy does endure forever! Praise You, Lord, for being the Great Shepherd who knows how and where to lead. Praise Your Holy Name."

2 Chronicles 20:21-22

Rejoicing with praise of God releases Him to work with a free hand—and eliminate that which otherwise would destroy. Focus on God. Worship and praise Him!

"Lord, I am so grateful for Your mercy and lovingkindness which is from everlasting to everlasting. What a relief it is to release all my cares to You, knowing You will give the victory!"

Grace Expressed Is Mercy Experienced, Part 4

Lamentations 3:21-33

This was written during the destruction of Jerusalem, God's judgment against the Jews. Jeremiah was mourning what could have been, grieving the ruin of Jerusalem, that once proud city. But in the midst of the judgment and destruction, tragedy was turned into triumph when the people took their focus off the situation and victoriously proclaimed the greatness of God's character.

"Lord, I want to always remember to allow You to turn tragedy into triumph by turning to You. You never change. You are consistent. Your holy love has to make 'tough choices', but I recognize that Your perfect love motivates every action."

Lamentations 3:21-33

We all go through personal struggles *BUT* God is still God! "Pour out your hearts like water before the face of the Lord." *(Lamentations 3:19)* "Let us search out and examine our ways and turn to the Lord, lifting our hearts in our hands." *(Lamentations 3:40)*

Tell Him your questions, struggles, and anxieties—cast your care on Him! Trust Jesus to reach out and touch your heart. Leave your problems with Him and then praise Him.

"Thank You, Lord, for being faithful! Thank You for listening and being the friend of a wounded heart. Your mercy and compassion heals and calms. You are all I need! Bless Your Holy Name."

Nehemiah 9

What a prayer! After the fall of Jerusalem and 70 years of captivity, the Jews were returning home, repentant, ready to respond to and worship the Lord. It was a time of repentance.

God's mercy is most obvious in history. The realization of His mercies in the past gives hope and encouragement for tomorrow.

"Lord, the recognition of Your work in the history of my life enables me to face tomorrow. Your grace, mercy, and love have taught me to honor You with all my heart! You are wonderful, my Lord and my God!"

Nehemiah 9

Where are you now, spiritually? Questioning? Rejecting? Committed wholeheartedly, but wanting a fresh touch? Are you in need of reassurance of His faithfulness? Do you need encouragement? Courage?

If any of these descriptions fit you, try worshipping Him. Express to Him His greatness and experience not just the joy of His presence, but also of the weight being lifted off your shoulders! Be refreshed by His Spirit.

"Blessed be Your glorious name, Lord. You alone are God. You are creative, loving, and merciful. You are faithful, trustworthy, and true. You are righteous in all Your ways, abundant in kindness and gracious. Your mercy is expressed over and over in a variety of ways. You are amazing! I stand in awe, grateful for who You are and how You always love me. Bless You, my Lord and my God."

Nehemiah 9

Recognize that His great love is expressed in ways that will make us aware of who He really is. His mercy is reaching out to draw us safely under His protection.

"Thank You for loving me enough to constantly be reaching out to me. Thank You for providing protection for my soul. You are my Rock and my Fortress, my Protector and Shield, and I thank You!"

Isaiah 61:1-3

This is a prophecy about the coming Messiah, Jesus. Notice that He gives beauty for ashes, the oil of joy for mourning, etc. God is a God of new beginnings. When He buries the past, it becomes the fertilizer for a fresh start. Our sins are forgiven, forgotten, and they cannot condemn us anymore. God knows how to turn our sorrows into joy. He is amazing that way!

"Thank You, Lord, for being the God of new beginnings. Thanks for giving me beauty for ashes. Thank You for taking my brokenness and making something beautiful from it."

Isaiah 63:7-9

Recognition of who God is and what He has done is a significant key to enable us to worship Him. Tell others about who God is and what He has done for you. By talking about Him we gain a greater realization of who He is and what He has done!

"Lord, thank You for all You've done for me. Give me opportunities to talk about You in honest and straightforward ways that will touch others' hearts and inspire them to trust You!"

Discovering God's Character in the Broad Places

Psalm 25:4-5

We are a goal-minded generation. But have you ever reached a goal and found it to be anticlimactic? Why is that? The process of reaching the goal is what is invigorating and challenging and where the real purposes are discovered. Each new day is part of the process for new opportunities to discover the reality of God.

"Lord, teach me to appreciate the process of reaching new goals. Order my steps; establish my heart to delight in the preparation process of reaching goals. I realize that it is through that preparation process You teach me and reveal more of Your character."

Psalm 31:8

When I was a young girl our family lived in the Philippines. One day my mom and I took a bus trip through an area famous for mountains that had been terraced for rice fields. We traveled up there, together with chickens and pigs, in an open sided bus. The road was only a narrow, steep lane on the side of a mountain—very scary. Our very lives seemed to be held in the driver's ability to navigate such a treacherous road.

"Sometimes, Lord, I feel like I'm on a precipice with no place to go, ready to fall over the edge and crash in failure. But the reality is it's an opportunity to cling to You and let You establish my way. Thank You for always doing that."

Psalm 31:8

On that trip I remember when another bus came from the opposite direction. The driver backed down the mountain until he found a broad place to stop and let the oncoming bus pass. It was a harrowing experience for Mom and me, but the Filipinos took it in stride. So my image of a broad place is vivid! It really is a place of security—trust the driver to find that secure place!

"Lord, thank You for Your wisdom and grace that guides me always to secure, side places. I have nothing to fear about the process because You always protect me."

Psalm 18:19, 30-36

Many years ago I was in great turmoil. I had been in excruciating pain for a long time and the only way to correct it was through surgery. Even after the surgery I was so physically and emotionally weak that I thought I was losing my mind. It was a terrible time, *but* my fears came to an end when I read Psalm 18. I realized that even though I thought I would lose my mind throughout the physical and emotional healing process, God had *actually* "set my feet in a broad place." Through the process of healing, the Lord taught me invaluable spiritual principles and truths.

"Thank You, Lord, for the times that seem hard but are actually the broad places of security where we discover spiritual truths and realities. Thank You for being the Lord of the process."

Psalm 40:1-5

The miry clay of depression and hopelessness assaulted me daily during that recuperation period. I remember sobbing my heart out in frustration and feeling so alone, yelling out to God in desperation to help me. The Lord heard me and set my feet on the rock by teaching me spiritual truths such as, "we become like whom we worship." That's why writing about God's character has great value to me! We must know Him and worship Him because He really liberates our spirits and establishes our hearts.

"Thank You again, Lord, for loving me enough to constantly be reaching out to me. Thank You for providing protection for my soul. You are my Rock and my Fortress, my Protector and Shield, and I thank You!"

2 Samuel 22:17-20, 29-37

David's song of thanksgiving is repeated in Psalms. The Lord wants us to understand the importance of David's experience. The celebration is not for the finished product as much as it is for the process of achieving the finish line, where we discover daily victory! *The truth of the service station* (the truth that keeps us empowered to keep going) is we must act upon our knowledge of God's character and His principles and *not* respond emotionally to the feelings we have about our circumstances.

"Thank You, Lord, for the truths learned in the broad places You set us in through the process of living. Thank You for teaching me the truth of acting on godly principles instead of letting changing emotions rule me. You alone are my Lord and my God."

Psalm 118:4-9
Romans 8:37-39

Fear and faith cannot co-exist. Faith knows the truth that **God is on your side**! Fear is the enemy. Faith is a shield to protect you. Act on the truth of God's word. Trust Him with the outcome.

"Lord, I trust You and wait expectantly for You. Thank You for being the victor over all situations. You are my rock and my fortress! When I turn to You, I discover that wonderful truth!"

The Lord Listens To & Shelters the Wounded Heart

Psalm 61:1
Philippians 4:6-8

Have you ever said the words, "Listen to this!"? Or maybe, "Listen! I need to talk to you, right now!" Those words express the urgency of the moment. Haven't you at times in prayer cried out, "O God, hear my heart!" Filtering through the fallout of difficulties to the heart of the matter is the Lord's specialty. He sees, knows, and understands our hearts better than we do.

"Thank You, O Lord my God, for knowing and tuning into my heart, and loving me anyway. Thank You for listening wholeheartedly when I cry out to You in times of hurt, panic, fear, and overwhelming circumstances. You are always so good and gracious to me."

Psalm 61:2

In this verse, David declared his commitment to turn to the Lord whenever he felt overwhelmed by troubling circumstances. Can we take it one step further? What about the times we are overwhelmed with joy? Can we not run to God in those times as well? The commitment must be to turn to our Lord and God at all times, in all circumstances. Doesn't that equal "pray without ceasing?" *(1 Thessalonians 5:17)*

"Thank You, Lord, for being my Rock and my haven of rest in times of trouble. Thank You for rejoicing and singing with me in times of joy. Thank You for comforting me in times of confusion. You are always there for me! Amazing! The Almighty, Omnipotent Lord loves and cares for individuals so personally. I'm forever grateful!"

Psalm 61:3
Ephesians 3:14-21

The Lord generously protects and gives perspective to all who call upon His name. The Lord's shelter sometimes is inner security and peace as well as outward protection. But *always* He gives what we need in our present situation when we turn to Him!

"Thank You, Lord, for being my Rock on which I stand in the midst of uncontrollable circumstances. Thank You for Your peace, Your wisdom, and joy that gives a better perspective to what I'm facing. You are my strength and hope!"

Psalm 61:4
Proverbs 3:5-6

Our part in our relationship with the Lord is to honor, revere and worship Him in every area of our lives, seeking the intimacy of communing with Him—sharing our hearts, talking, listening, and growing closer daily. The Lord has done everything necessary to pave the way for us to grow close to Him. But He leaves the choice to us. Making this decision is an awesome responsibility for each one of us.

"Lord, I choose and determine to follow You as my Lord and my God with all my heart, mind, strength! I love how You love me. There is no place I'd rather be than in the shelter of relationship with You."

Psalm 61:5
Hebrews 12:1-3

Each of us has a rich heritage of faith. For some, it's a family member. For others it is a Sunday School teacher, Bible study teacher, missionary, friend, pastor—those people in our history and present who show us the truth of who God is. Or perhaps our faith is prompted by people we don't know personally: people in the Bible, or a Corrie Ten Boom, Charles Colson, Joni Ericson Tada, or others in modern history who witness to the reality of God in the midst of monstrous difficulties and in the victories they have experienced.

"Thank You, Lord, for the rich heritage of believers who inspire, encourage, and point me to You. May my life, in turn, be an encouragement to others as they see You at work in me and in my circumstances."

Psalm 61:6-7
John 8:31-32

The realization of the truth and mercy of God is what draws us to Him and stabilizes our faith.

Here in Japan, going to the "gas stand" is quite an experience. Not only do several attendants welcome you verbally, but they also tell you where to stop. They fill the car with gas, wipe the windows, offer to check the oil and empty your car trash. In that, they and treat you like an honored guest. It's wonderful! God's mercy and truth are like that; the "truth of the service station" is God's truth that keeps us going, rejuvenating and refreshing us.

"Thank You, Lord, for creatively finding ways to welcome each person into the joy of discovering Your grace and mercy. Thank You for the refreshment and rejuvenation Your Word and presence gives. You are so good to me!"

Psalm 61:8
Hebrews 13:15-16

Praise releases the Lord to work. Through praise, we focus on God, reminding ourselves of who He is and what He does. There is power in authentic, from-the-heart praise. That power works in our hearts and minds to release God's power in our lives. By focusing on Him and expressing His greatness, we are inspired to serve Him with gladness.

"You are worthy of praise, O Lord, not just for what You do, but for who You are. Your love, mercy, and grace draw me to You. Your peace and joy fill me with gratitude. You are totally amazing!"

God's Character of Righteousness

Psalm 33:4-5

We have reason to praise and worship the Lord. His Word is right, meaning "upright, honest, or honorable". Everything He does is done in truth and integrity. He is not capable of anything less than that. He loves righteousness and justice, for they are pure and honorable. The earth and our lives are abundantly full of His goodness and lovingkindness.

"Thank You, Lord, for the purity and honesty of who You are. Everything You do and everything You are is a pure expression of Your integrity, honorableness and grace—and I am blessed because of it! It's amazing that You are perfect love and yet reach out to imperfect me! Thanks. I'm grateful."

Psalm 45:6-7
Hebrews 1

This prophetic Psalm, quoted in Hebrews, describes how God the Father felt about His Son, Jesus. The scepter, a symbol of authority and power, is righteousness. The word "righteousness" is a noun that comes from the root word meaning "straight."

"Thank You, Lord, for Your righteousness. The purity and holiness of Your Lordship is awesome."

Psalm 45:6-7
Hebrews 1

Interestingly, the top-right part of the Chinese character for righteousness (儀), used also in Japanese, is the symbol for lamb (羊). The word for justice in Japanese has two characters (正義). The first one means "perfect"; the second one means "righteousness". We always need the Lamb to express righteousness and justice.

"Lord, we do need the Lamb of God to experience Your truth, justice and righteousness. It is through the death of Jesus, the Lamb of God, on the cross that payment was made for my sins—to satisfy Your righteousness, O God. Amazing perfection sacrificed Himself as an expression of love for imperfect me. Wow, Lord, I'm humbled and yet honored! How can I not respond to Your amazing love?"

Romans 3:21-30

It is amazing and wonderful! The Creator of the law and the Righteous Judge, knew there was no way we could obey His perfect law and meet the demands for righteousness. So, He made His omnipotent self vulnerable by dying in our place, paying our penalty for sin!

"Your love is amazing, Lord. You who knew no sin willingly sacrificed Yourself for me. It's humbling. But wonderful! Thank You. I'm so grateful for what You've done for me!"

Romans 3:21-30

Amazing! The standard bearer and judge of all that is perfect, true, and righteous became our Savior. Jesus paid the price and made the way clear for you and me, through our faith in Him, to stand righteous before God, the Father! Amazing!

"Lord, I sing the song, 'Amazing Grace'. But even having experienced salvation through faith in Jesus, I can't begin to comprehend what You have done for me. All I can do is humbly bow and gratefully worship You, my Lord and my God!"

Psalm 36:5-9

How can I write a commentary or even begin to express anything about these verses? What keeps us from experiencing the truth of these verses? Ungratefulness, unbelief, complaining, self-centeredness? Who wants to be like that? Let's rejoice and express our gratitude!

"Thank You, Lord, for being righteous. Thank You for Your mercy and faithfulness to me, who stands always in need of Your righteousness. Your lovingkindness is precious, and it is a joy and relief to put my trust in You."

1 John 2:1-2

We have an advocate, one who fights and intercedes for us! It is Jesus who embodies righteousness and conforms perfectly in thought, purpose, and action to the Father's standards. Jesus is not only our advocate. He is also the one who gave His all by paying the price for your and my sins so we might have relationship with God. He gave His all for us; why can't we give our all to Him?

"Lord, forgive me when pride stands in the way of my responding wholeheartedly to You. Lord, sometimes it's self-pity, feeling I'm not good enough for You, that keeps me from accepting Your sacrificial gift willingly provided for me. Clear my eyes and heart so I can humbly reach out and just accept what You have done."

He Is All Our Righteousness

Matthew 5:6
Isaiah 65:24

To hunger and thirst for righteousness is to truly recognize our need for the perfect righteousness of God. That will cause us to seek Him. God doesn't condemn us for our lack, but rather makes provision for us. We condemn ourselves when we reject Jesus and His holy sacrifice for us.

"Thank You, Lord, for seeing my need, hearing my cry and making provision for my sins. I gratefully accept Your precious gift of salvation. My choice is to worship You, the righteous, loving Lord of lords."

Matthew 6:33

Develop the skill of seeking God and His righteousness first, and wholeheartedly, and you will discover a purer and deeper sense of wholeness and peace. My husband and I have often said there is no picture or video—nothing—to adequately describe what living in Japan is like to someone who has never been in Japan. How much more is that true in trying to describe the truth, reality, and wonder of God's kingdom? While we are living, that kingdom is our hearts where God is King and Lord. Peace, joy, and His love are the environment! If you haven't experienced it yet, now is the time to reach out and accept Christ as Lord.

"Thank You for Your kingdom which satisfies the longings of my heart. Jesus, You are my Lord, my Savior, and my King. I rest in Your peace and love. Bless Your Holy Name!"

Acts 10:34-43

Peter, who had denied Christ because of his fear of the unknown, discovered the reality of Jesus' love and forgiveness. He preached this message of truth for *all* peoples of *all* nations. God shows no partiality. Yes, He is holy and righteous. But His love is for *ALL*—a free gift. Have you accepted His gift of salvation yet? Jesus came to give us abundant life. We surrender pride, selfishness and other sinful actions to receive a rich, full, abundant life! Go for it! It's a joy!

"Thank You, Lord, for the new, abundant life Your sacrifice provided for me. I know I'm a sinner saved by grace and because of Your loyal love. I'm grateful!"

Romans 3:21-26
Colossians 1:15-23

*A*ll have sinned. No one can touch the glory, the righteousness, and the perfection of God. We can't earn it by works. We can't achieve it by action—it's humanly impossible. Only Jesus could pay the price for our righteousness. The one and only thing we can do is, by faith, believe and accept God's gift of salvation.

"Thank You for Your gift of salvation. Thank You that surrendering my pride and self-focus to You only leads to absolute victory, complete joy and peace. You are wonderful in all Your deeds, O Lord, my God."

John 19:28-30

All looked hopeless. It appeared a good man had died unjustly on that dark Friday. But the truth was, by dying on the cross, Jesus completed the work needed to pay the price so people could freely receive not only salvation, but also His righteousness. It was indeed Friday, but Sunday—resurrection day—was coming.

"Lord, You know my life sometimes seems difficult. Remind me that it's Friday, the day when hope seemed to die—but that Sunday is coming! Thank You for completing the work on the cross. Thank You for suffering indignity and abuse for me. And thank You for righteousness Your death and resurrection provided for me."

2 Corinthians 5:18-21
Romans 5:17-21

Why is there such a battle between creationists and evolutionists? The theory of evolution contradicts the Garden of Eden—and Adam and Eve's sin which, in turn, denies God's promise of a Savior. By one man sin entered the world. Have you ever thought that if circumstances were better, then you'd be better? Think about Adam and Eve—perfect environment, perfect relationship with God—and they still chose to sin! The choice is always yours! God chose from the foundation of the earth (*Romans 13:8*) to make a way for us to come into relationship with Him.

"Thank You for Your marvelous plan of salvation, Lord! Knowing mankind's weakness, You made a way to give us Your strength, Your righteousness, and abundant life. You are amazing!"

Luke 24:1-8, 38-53

Friday, all seemed lost and hopeless. But before there could be resurrection, there had to be death. It was a necessary death—the price love paid for you and me to enter into relationship with the righteous, holy God.

"Thank You for resurrection power! Jesus, thank You for paying the price for me and for the victory You freely give to each person who believes in You. You are more than wonderful. I stand in awe and worship You, my Lord and my God."

We Have a Living, Victorious Lord

1 Corinthians 15:3-7
Isaiah 53:4-12
Psalm 16:10

Jesus was not a martyr; He is a victor over death and sin. The gift of salvation and righteousness is because of Jesus' victory over death. His resurrection power is the same power He freely gives us to enable us to be overcomers in all situations!

"Thank You for Your victory that you willingly and unselfishly give to us because of Your unfailing love. I'm grateful!"

1 Corinthians 15:12-19

The resurrection is the pivotal point of faith. Without the resurrection, Christianity would be a dead religion like all other religions. But, as Christians, we worship a living, victorious Lord.

"Lord, I'm so grateful that believing in You, I serve a risen, living Lord, that I'm not trying to honor a dead person. What joy, what freedom, and what liberty You have given so generously! I stand amazed and worship You, O my Lord and God!"

1 Corinthians 15:20-28

Not only do we serve a risen Lord and Savior—but He is also coming again! We don't know when, but we have the blessed hope of His return in triumph. His first coming was as the suffering servant, our servant-King who humbled Himself and gave His all so we could be saved. The Second Coming will be as the Victor, returning in triumph.

"Lord, I'm looking forward to Your Second Coming. Come soon, Lord Jesus."

Acts 1:1-11
1 Thessalonians 4:16-18

His resurrection power enables us to proclaim the truth of the Gospel. The Holy Spirit empowers and teaches our hearts the absolute truth of who Jesus is. When we face spiritual battles the Holy Spirit enables us to learn more truth about who the Lord is what He has done. So when all is said and done, our victory is through the resurrection power.

"Thank You, Lord, for being the victor! Thank You for the Holy Spirit who teaches, enables, and empowers us. You are so good to those who trust in You. Thanks!"

John 14:1-4

When you truly trust the Lord, His Second Coming is a comfort— the blessed assurance. I don't know the "ins and outs" of it all, but I can join with Paul and say, "I know whom I have believed and am persuaded that He is able to keep what I have committed to Him until that Day!"

"Lord, I am so grateful, not just for Your being a living, victorious Lord, but also because You are faithful and trustworthy. What a joy it is to know You!"

Matthew 25:34
Mark 16:15-16

There will be a time of judgment separating believers from unbelievers. This will be heartbreaking for those who have refused to accept or believe in Jesus and do not have a personal relationship with Him. For this reason, we must share our faith by word and deed. Share the truth and the joy. Let your life be a light that reveals the reality of Jesus!

"Lord, open my eyes to see the opportunities to share Your truths. May my heart and life always reveal the same degree of compassion and grace as You have generously given to me."

Matthew 16:24-27
Philippians 2:5-11

In America we so often hear, "Do your own thing," or "Take care of #1 (*self*) first", keeping people from seeking Christ. In Japan, there are ways of speaking to intimidate people from seeking Christ. The cultures of the world each put pressure on people <u>not</u> to believe. Jesus says to deny those things that would separate us from Him. Don't try to fit into a culture that squeezes God out! Die to self just as Jesus did on the cross. Follow Him and discover true victory.

"Thank You, Lord, for exampling how to die to self. Thank You for coming as a man so You understand our struggles. Thank You for the grace to live the life You call us to live. Thank You for the victory of the cross! I'm so glad that I serve a risen Savior! "

Merciful Forgiveness, Marvelous Forgetfulness, Part 1

2 Samuel 11:1
Jeremiah 17:9-10

What is the first stepping-stone on the path to sin come from for believers? The stepping-stones of compromising standards and neglecting responsibility are two of the biggest temptations down the path that takes us away from God. Satan tempted Jesus to compromise God's truth and neglect His responsibilities. (Matthew 4:1-11)

"Merciful Lord, open my eyes and understanding to the areas of my life where I compromise Your truth as well as where I neglect to be and do what You have designed for me to be and do."

1 John 1:7-9
Psalm 51:1
Isaiah 43:25

Read 2 Samuel 11 through 12:24 for the history behind this Psalm. No one is perfect! We humans fail, we compromise, and we sin. Where is our hope? How can we be clean? Through repentance and confession. Repentance begins with being sorry for what you did—not sorry you were caught! That proceeds to confessing to the Lord what you did. Then you can experience the joy of forgiveness and God's merciful forgetfulness!

"Thank You, Lord, for Your merciful forgiveness and marvelous forgetfulness. Such non-condemning love is beyond my comprehension but I am overjoyed that I don't have to understand it all to receive the benefits of the double M-F phenomenon!"

Psalm 51:2
1 John 1:7-9

After working hard, sweaty and dirty, do you go to the mirror, turn around three times and say, "I wish I were clean, I wish I were clean, I wish I were clean."? If you do, you probably are still quite dirty—not to mention smelly—like *putrid*! You shower to wash away the dirt and you achieve cleanliness, right?

Since only the Lord can cleanse us from sin, why would we want to take our sins anywhere but to Him?

"Thank You, Lord, for not just Your incredible double M-F phenomenon, but also for Your cleansing work in us—with it."

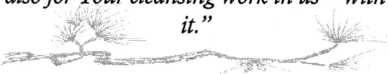

Psalm 51:3-4

Acknowledging sin is *so* hard. Our pride wants to say, "I just goofed a little." Or, "Oops, I stepped on the compromise stepping-stone again." But true repentance recognizes and acknowledges the sin, its consequences, and the pride and rebellion in us that expressed itself against God.

"Thank You, Lord, for being a just and righteous God. Thank You that I can throw myself on Your marvelous mercy and be forgiven and cleansed."

Psalm 51:5-6
Romans 5:12

We are all born with a sin nature. Our saving grace is from the Lord. Truth and wisdom come from what's inside us, not from some personal outer effort. As we reach out to Him more and more, receiving His forgiveness, His mercy, and His righteousness and all the benefits He alone can give, then we discover the deposits of truth and wisdom His presence always provides.

"Thank You, Lord, for generously and graciously giving truth and wisdom to all who seek You! Your touch is more than refreshing. It gives incredible benefits! I'm forever grateful!"

Psalm 51:7

Hyssop was used in ceremonies of purification in the Old Testament. Therefore David related hyssop to cleansing. Hyssop, being related to marjoram, combines the sense of smell and taste with sight to bring us such a complete reminder of God's cleansing power.

The amazing thing about David was that he was aware that real cleansing was not ceremonial, but the inner work of God.

"Thank You, Lord, for using all of our senses to bring reminders of the wonderful work You do in our hearts and lives."

Psalm 51:7

Is there anything more beautiful than fresh-fallen, pristine, white snow? When we follow the stepping-stones away from God, our hearts feel more like well-tracked, dirty snow. But God's cleansing work purifies and restores, making the condition of our hearts in reality whiter than snow. He does the work needed when we turn to Him with brokenness over our sin.

"Lord, thank You for restoring me when I am lost on the wrong path. You are always the source of meeting all my needs and questions. I am humbled, and yet blessed by Your great love! "

Merciful Forgiveness, Marvelous Forgetfulness, Part 2

Psalm 51:8-9, 103:11-14

The Lord is amazing. He doesn't just heal our brokenness. He exchanges our brokenness, dirt, and ugliness for joy, wholeness, beauty, peace, and purity— and He feels that is a good exchange!

What do we have to loose when we turn ourselves over to God? Only the awful, "yuckiness" of our lives and we gain the beauty and purity only God can give.

"Wow, Lord, how amazing is Your grace! It astounds me how You take our ugliness and freely give Your loveliness! Is this where the saying, "confession is good for the soul" comes from? How true!"

Psalm 51:10-11

So far in David's confession, he has asked God to 1) purge—to remove undesirable thoughts and ideas; 2) wash—cleanse and purify the filth of sin; 3) exchange—the condemnation he hears all around him for joy and gladness; and 4) blot out—obliterate His wrong actions. After David's requests, he cried out to Creator God to create a clean heart in him so he could dwell with the Lord.

"Oh, can I say thanks to You, O Lord my God, for all the work You do for me when I confess my sin to You! Your conviction leads to repentance. Then You provide all I need for wholeness! You are wonderful, Lord. I am so grateful to You for all You do for me!"

Psalm 51:12

David's next plea is for restoration. God is in the restoration business! Not only is He Creator God, but He is also the Restoring God! There's no need too great or hard that He won't be able to bring complete restoration to all those who call upon Him.

"Thank You for being not just Creator God, but also the God who restores. The entirety of Your forgiving work is almost too great to fathom. However, just accepting it without completely understanding it is a phenomenal experience. Thank You, my Lord and my God!

Psalm 51:13

W hen all our rotten, horrible, miserable experiences are given to God, then we experience His "double F-M phenomenon" birthed by His unconditional love. As a result, we want to tell others the joy of being forgiven. When they see in us the incredible work of God, we can become lights to reveal the Lord.

"O Lord, may my life shine with Your glory, revealing to others the wonder and joy of knowing You!"

Psalm 51:14-15

When we experience deliverance from sin, we recognize the God of our salvation. That realization is the birthplace of our awareness of God's righteousness and His amazing grace. That reality can do nothing but produce praise and thanksgiving.

"O Lord of my salvation, words of gratitude fail me. There is just no way to tell the beauty, relief and liberty of Your 'double M-F phenomenon'! Somehow use this understanding to create praise flowing from every aspect of my life."

Psalm 51:16-17

It isn't what we do that "earns" God's grace. It is in giving our hurt and brokenness to God that we freely receive His grace. Why does man persist in trying to earn God's love?

The only thing I know that comes close to this unmerited favor is when my children and grandchildren were born. They could cry, wet, mess, and demand food. Despite those actions, I loved (and still love) them and thought (and still think) they were wonderful and I happily served them. God's amazingly pure love is even greater than that of a mother or grandmother! Fantastic, isn't it!

"Lord, thanks for loving me so much! It's a relief and joy to give You my brokenness and hurts and then receive all the benefits of Your grace."

Psalm 51:18-19

After King David experienced the wholeness that comes from receiving forgiveness, he reached out in prayer on behalf of the people of his nation, Israel. He realized that his sin had affected these individuals, as well as himself. When we sin, it affects us as well as all those with whom we are connected. It's an awesome responsibility!

"Lord, thank You for those You have entrusted into my care. I pray that You will be seen in me and that Your 'double M-F phenomenon' will bear fruit—not just in me but in others as well. Bless Your Holy Name. "

The Blessings of God's DBL M-F Phenomenon

Psalm 32:1, 103:1-5

The person who has repented and confessed to the Lord knows only the blessing of forgiveness, whereas the unrepentant heart gets darker, heavier and colder. We make a personal choice to receive the blessings of forgiveness or to spiral downward in the negative consequences of the lack of repentance.

"Thank You, Lord, for the blessings You bestow on the repentant heart. Thank You for covering our sins. Thank You for being so gracious and wonderful!"

Psalm 32:2

Isn't it amazing how, when the Lord forgives us, He never mentions our sin again or charges us the price of forgiveness? Jesus paid it all! As we get to know Him in all circumstances, we should seek to learn how to have His openness with others, without hidden agendas. As we are blessed by His love, our motivation should be to pass the blessing on!

"Lord, teach me to be as guileless as You! Purify my motives as You cleanse my heart! Thank You for being a faithful, consistent teacher."

Psalm 32:3-4

Confessed sin brings blessing but unconfessed sin brings heaviness. When my niece and I were little girls, we discovered a gumball machine that gave "free gumballs" (*it was broken!*). Being penniless, we helped ourselves until pockets and cheeks were bulging with gumballs. For a moment they tasted good and we were delighted. But then our guilt over having stolen the gumballs weighed us down. We ended up running to the bathroom, depositing chewed *AND* unchewed gumballs in the toilet, praying and repenting. Cute story? Sure. But I remember vividly the joy of forgiveness even for a 9-year-old.

"Thank You, Lord, for the lessons learned, even as a child, about the blessings of forgiveness!"

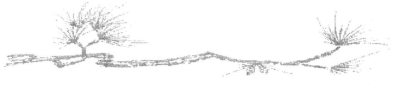

Psalm 32:5
Proverbs 3:3-5

As we release our past in our confession and repentance, we receive the healing balm of God's forgiveness, He brings wholeness in our hearts, minds, and emotions. Why would we not want to give it all to the Lord?

"Thank You for teaching us, Lord, not just through personal experiences, but also through others like David. I'm so glad You didn't whitewash the people in the Bible but let us see them 'warts and all' so we would know more of the wonder of Your mighty love and amazing grace."

Psalm 32:6-7

Problems we have and trouble we experience are the tools God uses to draw us close to Him. The place of security and safety is in relationship with the Lord.

"Thank You Lord, for nestling me close to Your heart, singing over me. You truly are my hiding place!"

Psalm 32:8-9

This is God's response to David. Read these two verses over and over and hear the Lord speak to *your* heart.

"Lord, I remember the first time I read these verses and realized how stubborn and hardheaded I am. O Lord, take my stubbornness and let it be used to keep me clinging to You instead of opposing You! My desire is to always seek You first!"

Psalm 32:10-11

Rejoice in God's gracious mercy. God pays the highest dividends of joy, peace, grace, and love when we simply believe and trust Him!

"Thank You, Lord, for Your graciousness. You are so good to me. I love the way You love!"

Faithfulness

Psalm 31:19-24

Our Lord is faithful. He stockpiles blessings to give us when we seek Him; He hides us in the secret place of His presence as we run to Him when the storms of life seem to toss about. God's love is a WONDER!

We must love, trust, and worship Him with our whole heart. He is faithful to the faithful. Even when we get discouraged and forget to turn to Him, He hears and understands. He takes care of His kids! So remember—Be brave. Be strong. Never give up. Oh, we must remember to respond to His love. Hope in the faithful Lord.

"Thank You, Lord, for Your faithfulness. Lord, I want to return the honor You have given me by being a faithful child. Thank You for strengthening my heart and enabling me to be faithful to You. You are so good to Your kids!"

1 Corinthians 1:4-9

We have access to God through Jesus Christ. We witness the evidence of God's faithfulness to us in His gift of His Son, Jesus Christ. We don't need a thing. Our Heavenly Father also freely gives us other gifts as we worship Him.

Not only that, but God upholds us and keeps us steady. He is ALWAYS faithful! He will never give up on you!

"Lord, Your generosity overwhelms me! You give and give and give to Your children. Thank You for Your generosity and faithfulness. Your grace, love and tender mercies give "go" power so faith can grow strong. Thanks. Lord!"

Psalm 92

W e need to look to the future by faith, remember the past to praise Him for His faithfulness. This enlarges our praise and gives it more dimensions as we recognize and acknowledge His sovereign Lordship. Looking to the past should never be to glory in the "good ol' days", but rather to give glory to God for His faithfulness. That's what builds hope and faith for the future.

"Lord, what a beautiful thing it is to give thanks to you! To declare your lovingkindness and faithfulness throughout the day, keeps me focused on you. Your joy overflows me. I'm amazed at your works and ways, O Lord! Your thoughts are simply too wonderful for words. Only fools don't recognize it. You are stronger than evil. Yea! And you make me strong. Your promises maintain my hope. You are my rock and my holy, righteous, ever faithful life preserver! Thanks!"

Psalm 23

God is my shepherd. He takes care of me. He is faithful to His word and gives me rest and peace, and gives me direction. I need not fear for He is with me and I feel secure.

"Lord, You feed me right in front of the trouble-makers in my life. All my days are filled with your presence. Your goodness and mercy follow in the wake of your leadership. Forever together—AMAZING!!"

John 14:1-4

Our blessed assurance. Not only is the Lord with us as we face our daily circumstances, but He is also preparing a place for us to come to. He is ever faithful to meet our needs now as well as in the unknown future.

"Thank You, Lord Jesus, for explaining to Your disciples so I can more clearly understand. Thank You for Your patience to answer questions and clear up our limited comprehension. But most of all, thank You for being the Way, the Truth, and the Life! Thank You for the power given to us in Your name. Thank You for all Your preparation and Your work for us. You are so good and loving, it amazes me."

Hebrews 13:8

Jesus is always the same. He was faithful in the past, He is faithful in the present, and He will be faithful in the future. He is the Rock. He doesn't have mood swings or temper tantrums. He is the faithful, loyal, consistent, loving Lord!

"Thank You, Lord, for Your forever faithfulness. It makes me feel so secure and loved, knowing and experiencing the consistency of Your character."

John 4:23-24

Since worship incorporates thoughts, feelings and deeds, there are many expressions for it. Worship includes praise and thanksgiving. It is giving God our trust, faith, loyalty and commitment. It's a dedication of ourselves to Him, knowing He values our gift more than we do. It blesses us to worship. Our cares and concerns are lifted and given to Him. God becomes our focus and we are blessed by His presence. He overwhelms us with His faithful blessings, love, and joy.

"Lord, I want to worship You in thought and deed. I want everything within me to respond in reverent worship to You and I want my actions to be acts of worship to bring You honor and glory. Show me how to best honor and worship You, O Lord, my God."

Amazement at God's Glory

PSALM 92

As we look back over our lives, we can see God's hand and we praise Him for His faithfulness. As we look ahead by faith, we can praise Him because we know His love and faithfulness by experience. He is our Rock; nothing is stronger than the Lord.

"Thank you Lord, for Your faithfulness that is eternal. You are my Rock and the hope I have is in You. Your great faithfulness and mercy that I have seen in others and experienced myself are the foundation for facing each new day. Thank you for a new day and Your abundant grace to give me all that I need to face the challenges and joys just for today."

PSALM 93

God's majesty, His kingly greatness, is amazing. When we stop and think of all He has created, the varieties of flowers, trees, animals, and people—all the beauty—and our God is greater than creation! He is also true, holy, and faithful. And He loves you and me unconditionally! Our perfect God loves imperfect us. Amazing!

"Lord, You are amazing. You know how to love me in the ways I need to be loved! I am so grateful for all that You are and all that You do. But most of all, I am grateful for Your unending love. It is a joy and a blessing to respond to Your love by loving, respecting and worshipping You!"

PSALM 8

Praising the Lord encourages faith and hope. It strengthens us because we are grasping positive truth, rather than complaining and whining which only make us discouraged and depressed. Praise looks at the reality of who God is. The amazing thing is that the Lord has given dominion over His creation to mankind. We are important to God and He has a purpose for us to fulfill.

"O Lord, let me see things from Your perspective and find joy and delight in You even in the trials I face. Even when the difficulties of life seem to overwhelm me, I still know that You are unchanging and You are worthy of all praise and glory. Therefore, I choose to praise You no matter what the circumstances. Praising You elevates my perspective and lifts my spirits."

PSALM 19

The unspoken truth of God's glory is visible to those who look, *really* look, at creation. The heavens, the earth, and all creation continually reveal the majesty of God. The law of the Lord—the revelation of the Lord's ways—teaches us. The testimonies of the Lord are His signposts and point us in the right direction. The statutes of the Lord are like life-maps showing the way to have joy. The commandments of the Lord are His directions for our lives. Since God's reputation is 24-carat gold and comes with a lifetime guarantee, we can praise Him unconditionally. As we realize, *really* realize, His greatness, then we will want to choose to follow Him.

"Thank you, Lord, for the beauty of your creation. It is a revelation of Your creativity and imagination and inspires my faith. I love the variety and beauty of what You have created. You have provided all I need to enable me trust You. It is really incredible to experience and observe Your wondrous ways!"

MATTHEW 10:29-31

This majestic Creator God cares for even the littlest bird. But He cares even more for you and me. He even knows the number of hairs on our heads! We have great value to the Lord. Even though He wants us to follow Him, He sets everything before us and lets us choose whether or not we will. Jesus knows that it's not always an easy choice. That's why it is vital that we look at the big picture of who God is.

"Lord, I love how You love me! It brings a smile to my heart and is the source of security that I feel deep in my soul. Thanks!"

JOHN 3:16-17
ROMANS 5:8

God's immeasurable love to us is seen in the life, death and resurrection of the one-of-a-kind life of Jesus. Jesus came, not to point fingers at us and tell us how bad we are, but to offer to help us, to love us, to give us victory over difficulties. We don't have to be good enough. We must simply believe the truth.

God loves you and wants you in His family.

"Thank You, Lord, for salvation and for giving resurrection power to us so that we can be victorious over the difficulties in life. It is a wonder and a treasure that I cherish, You cannot be praised or thanked enough for all that You do to express Your wondrous love!"

JUDE 20-25

Build yourself up in this holy faith, stay in the center of God's love, and always look for His mercy. Go easy on those who struggle. Be tender and love the sinner while hating the sin.

We can stand in wonder and appreciation for what Jesus has done for us, and know we are given His power and strength for our daily lives so He can proudly present us to the Father when we meet face to face.

"O Lord, our Lord, how excellent is Your name in all the earth! Teach me Your ways and show me how to reveal Your wondrous love and grace to others so they may have the joy of knowing You as well."

O LORD, our Lord, how excellent is Your name in all the earth!

The Goodness of God

PSALM 27:1-2

God's goodness is multi-faceted. It includes righteousness, holiness, justice, kindness, grace, mercy, and love. It has a purity that we humans can't comprehend. God's goodness shines as a beacon in a dark world as well as a light within our hearts. It provides the strength we each need to face daily challenges.

"Lord, I am grateful for Your goodness. Thank You for Your salvation which takes me from darkness into Your light. Lord, I pray that my life will reflect Your goodness in all that I do and say."

PSALM 27:3-4

When our eyes are not on the Lord, then what people around us say and do affects and influences us, often making us afraid to trust God. But if we are really seeking God, desiring to know Him and requesting to truly experience His presence daily, then our eyes are not on negative influences, but are completely focused on receiving more of God's goodness.

"Lord, I not only desire to behold Your loveliness, but to absorb it so Your beauty will be seen in me."

PSALM 27:5-6, 32:7

Security in troubled times is found in relationship with the Lord. Many years ago when our children were very young, we lived in a neighborhood where our neighbor hated Christians. She had a strong personality and soon influenced everyone to avoid us. The hate was tangible; even our children felt it. It was a lonely, isolated, and confusing time at first.

But through it all, I discovered that I had a safe, secure hiding place in the Lord. Later, another neighbor told me how sorry she was for her part in it. She had seen the love of God in our lives through our responses, and she became a very committed Christian.

"Thank You, Lord, for being a safe harbor for me when I am overwhelmed by circumstances. You have always been there for me. You truly are my hiding place!"

PSALM 27:7-8

To seek God's face requires a personal involvement. God doesn't want our Relationship with Him to be long distance.

We live across an ocean and half a continent from our grandchildren. Pictures we receive from them, cute as they are, are one-dimensional. But when we hold and interact with each grandchild, a special bond is developed. In the same way, only more so, unity and harmony develop when we seek God's face.

"Lord, I will seek Your face so I can know You intimately and draw closer and closer to You! Thank You for also seeking a relationship with me!"

PSALM 27:9-10

Sometimes, when we look at our inner self, we don't like what we see, so we wonder why God would want to know me and spend time with me.

But the real truth is that God knows you better than you know yourself and He still loves you. He is truly the perfect (Heavenly) Daddy.

"Thank You for Your 'forever' and complete love, Father. You who knows me best loves me most—faults and all. Amazing love! I am relieved and grateful."

PSALM 27:11-12, 25:4-5

Hopefully, the cry of our heart is, "Teach me Your ways." Learning God's ways opens the door to experiencing and expressing heavenly culture on the earthly plane. Seeking to wholeheartedly learn the joy of responding as He would liberates us from the frailty of human resources into the freedom of God's limitless resources.

"Thank You Lord, for being just not only an excellent, but a willing teacher as well. Open my heart, mind, and understanding to learn Your ways."

PSALM 27:13-14

Belief and hope are essential ingredients for our survival. They protect and preserve us, especially through difficulties. If it feels like the winter of your soul, wait, hope and believe that the Lord will bring a beautiful springtime. Once you have experienced this season of new life, reach out and encourage others who are struggling through difficulties.

"Thank You, Lord, that You always, faithfully, deliver us through the challenges of life. Open my understanding to see dark tunnel experiences as the challenges I need to increase my faith and find my hope in You."

God's Goodness: A Promised Provision

PSALM 31:1-4

There is only one totally secure place to put our trust...the Lord. Our hopes, dreams, feelings, emotional and mental health invested in the Lord are not just a security, but they also reap dividends of blessing.

Do you keep your money in an open box outside the door to your home? No? Why not? It's not secure! Right? We feel secure putting our money in a bank—that sometimes fails—yet we often leave our "precious" emotions and spiritual well-being unguarded and vulnerable.

"Lord, thank You for being my secure, solid rock of compassion and understanding. When I fail, when I hurt, when I have dreams and hopes, You not only listen, but You encourage and bless. You are awesome!"

PSALM 31:5-8

This is God's wonderful provision of a broad place. After a very difficult year of physical problems, I was an emotional basket case. It was horrible. But in that traumatic year I learned certain truths. "We become like whom we worship" and "trust what you know is truth and don't react to your feelings—but choose to respond to the truth." At the end of the year (after reading in Psalms about God's divine broad place), I realized He'd held me secure when I thought I would lose my health and emotional well being.

"Thank You, Lord, for being a God of truth and faithfulness. I know from experience that You preserve and keep me secure. I am now, and will continue in the future to be, glad and rejoice in Your mercy and steadfast love!"

PSALM 31:9-14

When do we doubt and waver in our faith? When our eyes are on the situation, not on God. We cannot understand all our circumstances. But in God's secure broad place, He teaches us and leads us in ways that are beyond our understanding. TRUST HIM—and do what you know to do!

"Thank You, Lord, that my times, events, and circumstances are in Your hands. I trust You, for You are my Rock and my Redeemer."

PSALM 31:15-18

Al of us, at one time or another, have been the object of gossip and sometimes even slander.

When that happens, what do we do about it? Anger doesn't solve anything. Hurt feelings don't solve the problem either. Gossiping in return drives us to the low level of those who slandered us in the first place. Go to God. Tell Him how you feel and ask Him to vindicate you. Then live your life with honor, proving the slanderers wrong. Live in the strength of God's grace.

"Thanks, Lord, for silencing lying lips. But more than that, thanks for Your grace that gives me the strength and courage to live a life by Your righteous principles."

PSALM 31:19
ROMANS 15:13

We cannot exhaust God's goodness. Remember that goodness includes righteousness, holiness, justice, kindness, grace, mercy, and love, which available in abundance for our daily needs. Reach out and claim what you need for today.

"Thank You, Lord, for always being there for us abundantly— providing all that we need for each day."

PSALM 31:20-22

The secret to discovering of all God has for us is to spend time in His presence. How one does that doesn't matter. Whether we are in the kitchen, the car, or outside, our prayer life isn't limited. We can sing or listen to worship songs as well. Even reading and meditating on His word can be done. Write down one special verse and think about it. In these, and in other creative ways, we can find God's presence wherever we are!

"Lord, show me how I can practically and creatively enjoy Your presence throughout the activity of my day. Thank You for Your goodness that is mine to use each minute of every day. Teach me how to do it for Your name's sake."

PSALM 31:23-24

Be strong and have courage. God's goodness never fails! Our hope is based on the truth and security of God's goodness that He gives uniquely to each of us for our own special circumstances.

"Thank You, Lord, for Your great love for each person. Thank You for Your eternal generosity. You are wonderful. I am humbled and in awe of Your love!"

God's Goodness Endures

PSALM 52:1
ROMANS 12:21

God's goodness is eternal and durable. No man and no situation can overpower the goodness of God. Even in the darkest times, there is no pit so deep that God's goodness is not deeper still. Focus on Him and find the light.

"Thank You, Lord, that Your goodness endures forever. Thank You for the strength and power of Your goodness. Lord, strengthen me in Your goodness so I can overcome by Your grace and respond in ways that will glorify You."

PSALM 52:2-7

It is good to know wickedness isn't as strong as God's goodness. The wicked will be destroyed and righteousness will shine forth.

I read a story about a member of the KGB in the former USSR who was on a squad whose whole purpose was to search out and destroy home churches. As he entered one home church he saw a beautiful young woman. He couldn't understand why she was there. The KGB members brutally beat all the people. A week or so later, the KGB squad went to another home church and that beautiful young woman—still black and blue—was there. Her testimony of faith haunted the KGB man. A couple of years later he also became a Christian because he saw the strength of God's goodness in that young woman and others. Although beaten, those Christians blessed him and did not curse him.

"Lord, may Your grace and goodness strengthen me to stand strong in times of distress and be a blessing."

PSALM 52:8-9
2 CORINTHIANS 1:3-4

God makes us flourish and be fruitful as we trust Him through the various situations and times of our lives. Learning to wait in hope and expect God's goodness to teach us to live our lives by His principles is faith in action! We also need to seek out other believers and encourage then as well as be encouraged ourselves!

"Thank You, Lord, for the family of believers who encourage one another. Thank You for Your many blessings in my life. You are wonderful!"

PSALM 23:1-3

The Lord leads each of us. He is the Good Shepherd. He is constantly caring for our hearts and souls, healing our hurts and bruises! God is so good!

"Thank You, Lord, for always leading us where You can provide all that we need. Each new day brings me new discoveries and adventures in faith! You truly are the Good Shepherd."

Psalm 23:4-5

To have a shadow, you must have light. God is the light and, therefore, is our source of strength during times of struggle. Look to the light to find your way!

"Thank You, Lord, for being the Light. You are my comfort in all situations. I fear no evil because You are my source of strength and lead in righteousness."

PSALM 23:6

Remember that God's goodness and mercy are the guardians that hold us so we can dwell in His presence today and forever.

"Lord, thank You for Your blessing me with the twin guardians of goodness and mercy. They provide all I need to support and encourage me. You are awesome, my Lord and my God."

ROMANS 2:4

God's goodness leads to repentance. Think about it! God's goodness experienced ourselves, and observed in others, touches and changes our life like nothing else can!

"Thank You, Lord, for Your goodness that I have experienced. Shine through me so others can see Your goodness in me, and come to know the joy of knowing You!"

The Key to Wisdom & Understanding

PROVERBS 9:8-10

To become wise, first we must be teachable. Tenderness and respect towards the teacher are essential ingredients in being teachable. Wisdom begins with recognition and response to the awesome, wonderful God above all gods.

"Holy God, what a wonder You are. You are morally pure and upright. In Your holiness I see Your wholeness and strength. Getting to know You is awesome. I'm so grateful for Your purity and wisdom. I thank You and bless Your Holy Name."

JOB 28:28
PROVERBS 1:7

As we honor God with our wholehearted worship, He does a cleansing work in us. When we respond to God's holiness, He starts revealing our motivations and gives us insight so we can have wholeness in our thought life and attitude.

"Lord, You know I need Your wisdom! Teach me to worship and honor You in spirit and in truth. Purify my thoughts, motives, and attitude. Be glorified, Lord, in my words and deeds."

PSALM 99:1-3

We all generally show awe in one of two ways: either by silence or by joyful exclamation.

I am an avid NBA basketball fan. My team is the San Antonio Spurs, yea! In the 1999 Western Conference finals, they played the Portland Trailblazers. With barely a second remaining in the third game the Spurs trailed by two points. In the last possible second Sean Elliott stood on his toes just inside the boundary (if his feet had been flat on the floor, he would have been out of bounds) and shot a 3-pointer. As the ball flew through the air, there was a collective hush. Then...swish...three points! And San Antonio won! The crowd went wild. Such jubilation!

In worship, there are times to stand in awe, marveling at God's magnificence. But there are also times to joyfully and enthusiastically proclaim who God is.

"Lord, when I think of Your holiness, I stand in wonder at Your purity. But when I recall what You have done in the past, it's with amazement and joyfulness that I proclaim Your love and faithfulness! You are more than wonderful!"

PSALM 99:4-9

Because the Lord is holy, He is fair and just. He is the righteous judge. It is hard as humans to understand unconditional love and righteous judgment because our motivation is not pure. We have a tendency to be selfish. But God loves us enough to correct and love us all at the same time. God's corrective love establishes boundaries that give us the freedom to "be" without the bondage of an uncertain and conditional value system.

"Lord, You are holy and awesome. Thank You for not only correcting me when I stray, but also for setting good, solid, righteous boundaries in which I can express myself freely. There is incredible, joyous freedom in knowing You!"

PSALM 111:1-6

God's nature is holy. There are no ethical or moral dark spots in Him, only purity. He sees through our impure motivations and control issues and wants to work in us to bring a purity of heart and soul that, in turn, brings wholeness, peace, joy, and light.

"Lord, thank You for Your holy and righteous standards. They bring unspeakable relief and joy. You are righteous in all Your ways."

PSALM 111:7-9

We can see God's nature in the principles of His Word. Everything He does is established in truth and justice. Everything about the Lord is trustworthy, whether we understand His ways or not. We need the understanding and wisdom to live a life based on His principles and Word, responding by faith to do what we know to do.

"Thank You, Lord, for being trustworthy and faithful. You are holy and righteous in all Your ways. I worship You, Almighty God, my Lord and King."

PSALM 111:10

Remember the basic truth: reverent, wholehearted worship of the Most Holy God is what establishes true wisdom. As we respond to our loving Lord, we are changed, cleansed and purified. He can make our hearts, minds and spirits clean and light.

"Thank You, Lord, for involving the whole person that I am, for cleansing me inside so I am set free from bondages and hurts. Praise Your holy name forever!"

Holy is the Lord

ISAIAH 6:1-4

The prophet Isaiah had a wonderful and unique experience. He saw the Lord. It didn't become a matter of pride or bragging. It just made him more aware of his own lack and, therefore, his need to humble himself before the Lord. He understood that to worship the Lord in spirit and truth was to realize and declare the holiness, sovereignty and glory of God.

"Lord, I know in my head the truth of Your holiness, sovereignty and glory. But I confess to You that I lose perspective on that truth, especially when faced with tough decisions and/or difficult circumstances. Help me, Lord, to keep that truth uppermost in my mind, spirit and heart so that everything I say and do will glorify You."

ISAIAH 6:5
1 PETER 5:6-7

The realization of God's purity and holiness reveals our own unrighteousness and impurity. Humbling ourselves is to know that in the light of God's glory, sovereignty and holiness we are sub-zero. We must acknowledge that truth, while lifting Him up to be our Lord and God. His love, goodness, mercy, and grace then raise us up, and He embraces us as His children.

"Lord, You are pure and holy, full of glory, and You reign in power and strength. I know how weak and unclean I am. Lord, I need You to be Lord of every area of my life."

ISAIAH 6:6-8
ROMANS 12:1-2

God wonderfully purifies and prepares us. He has tailor-made His call on our lives to fit us perfectly. Our greatest act of worship is to respond wholeheartedly to God's direction and call—even though we may feel inadequate. God's call is never separated from His grace and empowerment. He is the strong and yet generous One in this partnership. It is in His will that we discover His abundant blessings.

"Lord, through all the struggles and difficulties and challenges we have faced as missionaries, I have never felt bereft of Your grace and tenderness. I don't understand what tomorrow holds, but I know You do. So I put my hand in Yours. I trust You and go forward with the anticipation of discovering Your revealed will."

ISAIAH 57:11-13

What holds back our personal wholehearted worship of God? Fear of what others will think? Cultural bias? Personal pride? Self-centeredness? The desire to be in control of our destiny? God is faithful to strip us of all areas of false security so we can discover true security. The reality is that He is our safe harbor, the Lord of lords and God above all other gods.

"Thank You, Lord, for showing me that there is no security or protection apart from You. You are indeed my Rock and my Fortress. I trust in You because You are completely trustworthy. Your love and grace hold me securely. Your goodness and mercy surround me. You are a wonder! I'm so grateful for You!"

ISAIAH 57:14, 62:10

As we discover God's awesomeness, shouldn't we respond by letting His life and light shine through us so others can see the truth? When others experience who God really is by observing a lifestyle professing the fullness of God's grace, joy, peace, then the stumbling stones that keep them from believing are removed. Then, they can also experience the freedom of having the Lord Jesus as their personal Savior. So let's be rock-pullers!

"Lord, knowing You is the bedrock of my life. I am overwhelmed by Your awesome holiness, goodness, mercy, and love—the list is limitless. You are a wonder. Your purity is inconceivable. I want others to know this joy of knowing You. Shine, Lord Jesus, through me so all the rocks of unbelief in other's lives may be loosened and released from their hearts so the good seed of Your Word can be planted."

ISAIAH 57:75

Old Testament principles hold true through the New Testament right down to today and throughout eternity. One of these truths is that hearts that are humble before the Lord and see their personal need for the Holy God are the ones who open the door to Him and grow close to Him.

"Lord, may my heart ever be humble and tender before You. Open my eyes and understanding more and more to Your Holiness so that I might comprehend my ever-present need for You, my Lord and my God."

ISAIAH 6:3

Reread to remember that He is Holy! I can't totally understand it, but that doesn't devalue God's holiness. Try to realize that God has pure motives when He reaches out to us in unconditional love to embrace us and to draw us into a loving relationship with Him.

"Thank You, Lord, for love so great that You continually reach out to me to embrace me, warts and all. You are awesome!"

Declarations of God's Holiness

EXODUS 15:11-13

This is part of a song of victory after God miraculously delivered Israel from Egypt at the Red Sea. Victory songs recount the wondrous holiness and acts of God. The secret is to remember that we are led by mercy and lovingkindness and guided by His strength—all motivated by God's holiness.

"Who is like You, my Lord? Cement in my heart the truth of the songs of victory so that, in times of struggles or when leaps of faith are required, I will be able to walk in the truth with full confidence in You. You are glorious in holiness, awesome in splendor, doing wonders! Thank You!"

1 SAMUEL 2:2-3

This is a prayer of victory because the Lord fulfilled His promise to Hannah for her to have a son. She is rejoicing because of the fulfilled promise, but more importantly she is recognizing the unparalleled holiness of the Lord.

Last week we saw that Isaiah's recognition of God's holiness was both a humbling and a healing experience. This week we see people realizing God's holiness in victory. Songs of victory are wonderful, but it's 20/20 hindsight! What we need to remember is to have 20/20 faith for each and every circumstance we face!

"Lord, my desire is to rejoice in You—no matter what! Open my understanding of Your holiness to build my faith, as well as to celebrate the victories You give."

191

LUKE 1:46-48

Mary didn't understand how she, a virgin, could have God's Son, the promised Messiah. But the Angel of the Lord (Luke 1:37) said, "For with God nothing will be impossible."

Jeremiah wrote, "Ah, Lord God! Behold…there is nothing too hard for You." (Jeremiah 32:17)

Mary was in the midst of a miracle as she recognized God's greatness and the wonder of His holiness.

"Lord, the bedrock of faith in You is to comprehend that with You nothing is impossible and recognize the reality of Your holiness. You, Who are mighty, have done, and continue to do great things for me."

LUKE 1:49-50

The Almighty, Holy God has done great things! Matthew 5:3 says, "Blessed are the poor in spirit...." This means those who recognize their need for God and honor Him for His purity, majesty, glory, mercy, compassion, kindness, and goodness. When we realize our need for complete dependence on God, we will experience the strength and dignity of right relationship with the Lord and how to live and enjoy His kingdom here on earth.

"Thank You, Lord, for Your promises. Thank You for Your faithfulness. It is a joy knowing You because You are wonderful, the Righteous King, Holy and Just!"

LUKE 1:51-55

Isn't it amazing how Almighty God honors those who recognize their need and humbly seek Him! God's strength is reserved for those who recognize their need for Him.

Pride, self-righteousness and arrogance are walls we erect to exclude God from our lives. Why do we continually fail to deny our need for the Almighty, Holy God who loves us so completely?

"Oh Lord, I recognize the times I go off on my own independent way, not recognizing my need for You. Open my eyes to the temptations that distract me from You so I may stay in tune with You!"

PSALM 30:4-5

God's attribute of holiness should inspire us to respond and worship in awe. God's correction is for our own good and brings us joy! His holiness demands that He correct us, His children, because He knows that only then will we experience the fullness of His joy.

One time when our oldest son was about 11 years old, he was acting horribly. My husband and I agreed he was crying out for discipline. After he was punished, not in anger but in love, he was relieved and happy! God's correction is so we can experience the freedom of joy, not the bondage of self-centeredness.

"Thank You, Lord, for Your holy nature and for correcting me when I act unrighteously, so I can experience the reality of the joy You alone can give."

PSALM 97

Rejoicing needs to be unconditional. Are you facing a difficulty? In the midst of a struggle? Feeling like you're in a tunnel with no light at the end? At the end of a struggle? Rejoice! No matter what your circumstance is, God is always the same. We only have to think of Him to rejoice. Knowing He is holy, faithful, and loves you is great cause for rejoicing!

"Lord, may I always remember to rejoice in who You are. no matter what! Because the truth is that You are the holy, righteous, loving, Almighty God. Praise Your Holy Name!"

Responses to God's Holiness

2 CORINTHIANS 7:1

Because of who God is, as well as all He has done, we need to honor Him by choosing to illuminate areas in our lives which are "faith-shrinkers" or areas where we deny God access. Perfecting personal holiness is a choice we make as a gift to God, and our gracious Lord honors and enables us to become more like Him.

"Thank You, Holy Father, for all You have shown and exampled to me about living a life pleasing to You. Show me the areas in my life that still need to be cleansed. My desire is to be more like You."

1 PETER 1:13-16

Remember that Old Testament principles hold true even today. "Be holy, for I am holy" was an Old Testament command reiterated in the New Testament, and is still true today.

To worship the Lord in spirit and truth (action), we must choose to be set apart from the ordinary by living our lives by godly standards!

"Lord, show me how to conduct my life in a way that glorifies You. Enable me to retrain wrong thought patterns that result in actions which don't honor You. Teach me Your ways, O Lord, and show me Your paths."

1 CHRONICLES 16:8-9

How can we retrain wrong thought patterns? Follow the pattern David gives in this song of praise. 1) Be thankful and express it to the Lord. 2) Call on Him—ask, seek, and knock. 3) Tell others about our holy, awesome God. Be a signpost pointing to God in word and deed. Remember what He's done and rejoice!

"Lord, You are worthy of praise! I'm so grateful that You will be found by those who seek You. You deserve all the glory, for You are full of grace and love."

1 CHRONICLES 16:10-12

Seek God wholeheartedly and completely, directing your heart and soul to know Him. What do you think about? When you don't know which way to turn, to whom do you turn? Is your desire to know God determined or limited by friends?

"Lord, close my ears from any voice that distracts from You. Shut my eyes from anyone or anything that would detour me from knowing You more. I want to know You and worship You—and You alone!"

PSALM 29:1-2

Recognize what the Lord has done and express gratitude to Him as well as encourage others by telling them what He has done. Our lives should not just be "Sunday good," but all week long we must let God's grace shine in every area of our lives. Then we can experience the joy of "worshipping the Lord in the beauty of holiness."

"Lord, You know better than anyone else the areas in which I fall completely short of the ideal of holiness. Thank You for not condemning me, but for convicting me, bringing the healing I need. I confess my failure and receive Your forgiveness. You are a wise Father and teacher, and I completely trust myself to You."

ROMANS 12:1-2
EPHESIANS 4:23-32

The transformed mind. Wow! Heavy subject! Daily we are faced with choices of how to respond. We must choose to appropriate God's grace and strength to respond by Godly principles, rather than yield to temptations and react in the old ways. Many of those contrasting choices are listed in Ephesians. We actually live our lives one choice and experience at a time.

If we blow it—and we will—remember that by confession we are cleansed (1 John 1:9). It's all a process—it's not instantaneous!

"Lord, teach me how to walk daily in ways that please and honor You. Thank You for Your cleansing and forgiveness which always give me a fresh start."

1 CHRONICLES 16:28-29

What offering can we give the Lord that will express our worship of Him? Isn't it our thoughts, our hearts, our words and our lives? God gives us His best. He asks in return for us to respond to His love wholeheartedly.

"Lord, it's simply amazing to me that You, the holy, righteous, Almighty God want a relationship with me. How can I withhold from You any part of myself knowing Your motivation is pure and loving? Knowing all that, I still forget to do it sometimes. Thank You for being patient!"

The Holy God Must Discipline

PROVERBS 3:5-13

We often quote verses 5 and 6. But how often do we put those verses into context? We are challenged to learn trust in our daily circumstances through acknowledging our need for Him.

But how often do we reject the idea of being disciplined? Being teachable is a quality our holy God prizes. Will we trust Him enough to become teachable?

"Holy Lord, I realize because of Your pure and holy nature, You see how terrible sin really is. I realize that discipline is an expression of love. I am stubborn and self-willed. Forgive me and help me become teachable. Help me, O Lord, for I am weak!"

HEBREWS 12:5-13

My mom taught me that discipline was to serve several purposes. It is to 1) teach me to obey God, 2) serve as a deterrent for further unsatisfactory behavior, not as an expression of her anger, 3) to train and prepare me for adulthood, and 4) to make me sorry for my wrong, not just sorry I got caught. My very wise mom gave me an appreciation for wise discipline!

"Lord, thank You that You are a wise disciplinarian. You know how to correct, train, and discipline each person effectively, so each will learn to become conformed to Your will in purpose, thought and action. Your correction is really a blessing—even though during the correction, it doesn't feel like it. But afterwards, the results are a joy!"

PSALM 94:12-15

God's discipline blesses, teaches, and prepares us to pass the more difficult tests ahead. An athlete still works out in the off-season and practices so he or she can improve and be prepared for the next season. In the same way, we must also learn to be teachable and willing to be corrected so we can meet the challenges ahead with God's strength and with the endurance needed to persevere!

"Thank You, Father God, that Your precious Son, Jesus, also learned obedience through suffering (Hebrews 5:8). Thank You, Jesus, for identifying so closely with us that You <u>willingly</u> gave up everything so I can know that You understand. I recognize You and honor You for being my Lord and Savior."

REVELATION 3:19-22

Once, when our eldest son was about nine or ten years old, he took some candy from a store without paying. Fortunately I caught him and made him return it. Then he was restricted to his room for a week so he could understand the concept of prison. It was horrible and wonderful. He never forgot. My love for him motivated me to teach him the peril of wrong choices. God, our heavenly Father, is even more motivated than an earthly parent to teach us how to wisely choose our course of action!

"Thank You, Lord, that You teach with wisdom so that we can learn to be wise. Thank You for correction given in love that instructs me in righteousness."

2 CORINTHIANS 7:9-10

As a mom, I wanted to make sure my children were sorry they had disobeyed, and not just sorry they got caught! God, too, wants us to be sorry when we disobey. Godly sorrow for what we have done leads to true repentance. Godly sorrow isn't a hopeless feeling. It brings a sense of hope, a desire to repent and experience the joy of our salvation.

"Thank You, Lord, for Your conviction and correction are so healing. You know how to discipline wisely! Help me, Lord, to be humble and teachable before You!"

PSALM 51

This is a beautiful prayer of repentance by David. He was guilty of lust, which led from coveting to adultery, and that led to murder. But when God confronted him with what he had done, he humbled himself before God and repented. David had to pay the consequences of his sin, *BUT* the truly good news is that God called David "a man after My own heart who would do all My will"!

"Lord, make me strong enough to know my failings—and wise enough to humble myself before You. Create in me a clean heart and renew a steadfast spirit within me…."

ISAIAH 55:6-13

The result of confession and repentance is pardon and joy. Amazingly enough, the Lord doesn't merely forgive, but He also forgets! God's ways and thoughts are not ours. We have to trust Him to be God!

Children don't have an adult perspective or wisdom. Have you heard and/or said, "Because I'm Mom/Dad, that's why." Neither do we, as humans, have God's perspective or wisdom! Our job is to trust and obey.

"Thank You, Lord, that You are not limited to my human finite thoughts! Your ways aren't restricted to man's ways. You are wise, holy and full of goodness. What a relief it is to know that!"

The Righteous Judge

DEUTERONOMY 32:3-4

Toward the end of his life, Moses declared the character of God. Our God, Who is the Righteous Judge, can be trusted to have no ulterior or selfish motives. He is motivated by truth, justice, mercy, and unconditional love. He is constant. What a comfort it is to know He never changes and His compassion never fails!

"Lord, You are awesome and mighty. I have tremendous respect for Your holiness, righteousness, and sense of justice. But it's Your Fatherhood that comforts me most and fills me with joy. You, my Lord, know just how to meet me at the point of all my needs!"

PSALM 50:1-5

It is impossible for God to act unrighteously! His justice and rightness are declared through creation, as well as to mankind. I've written often of my mom. She was just in the boundaries she created for me, as well as in her training and discipline. If my mom could be so loving and yet strict as a human, how much more is God capable of exhibiting that to us! His immeasurable love, as well as justice, reaches out to touch our lives and teach us righteousness.

"Thank You, Lord, for my godly mom who taught me so much about You. Thank You for all the ways You teach me and direct my paths so I can know You and learn Your standards and principles."

PSALM 96:1-6

It is so wonderful how God's greatness is expressed in song! We can sing to our great God who creatively expresses Himself in so many ways to us. He is our Rock. He is stable, unmovable, and trustworthy—total security! It's truly awesome!

"Lord, You are completely honorable and strong. I love that about You! Teach me to live my life to display Your truth. You are a great and wonderful God!"

PSALM 96:7-10

What does "worship in the beauty of holiness" mean? I don't have all the answers. I'm still in a quest for more understanding. But notice the verbs preceding this statement. They instruct us to "give," "bring," and "come" (*NKJ version*). Throughout history God has been giving, bringing, and coming to us, so it stands to reason that our worship would respond to God and honor Him for the ways He has generously revealed Himself to us.

"Lord, teach me how to worship You in the beauty of holiness. I want to respond to You in ways that honor You and to declare Your greatness by word and deed."

PSALM 96:11-13

We can all rejoice and be glad that the Lord always has and will continue to judge in righteousness and truth. When we live our lives, motivated by love for and worship of God, we have no reason to fear His judgments!

"Lord, teach me to respond to You and to live in integrity. You are so awesome and wonderful. My heart's desire is to worship You with my heart, mind, and soul, and then let that flood over into my words and actions."

PSALM 98:1-9

As God's righteousness and justice are revealed, it is cause for us to sing for joy! Two of the facts that strike fear in our hearts when we contemplate facing judgment are: 1) when we're wrong and know it, and 2) when we feel the judgment is unjust, critical or accusatory. But God, our Righteous Judge, brings the best for us out of each of these circumstances—1) when I am wrong, His judgment produces healing and repentance in me. 2) He is incapable of being unjust, critical or accusatory.

"Lord, thank You for being righteous and just in all Your ways! Thank You for correcting me in ways that bring health to my spirit and heart. You are righteous and just. I feel safe and secure in Your hands. I love You, Lord."

PSALM 72:2-4

God reigns in righteousness and justice. He alone can be trusted to be the King of our hearts.

"Thank You for being pure and holy, righteous and just. The more I learn to trust You, the more I discover Your goodness, lovingkindness and grace. You alone are worthy of all praise and worship."

Recognizing the Value of God's Judgments

PSALM 19:1-6

Judgment isn't always passing sentence for guilt. Good judgment knows how and when to do things wisely and well. I love Psalm 19 for many reasons. This week let's read it with the awareness of the variety of ways God expresses incredible judgment in all His ways!

"Lord, I see Your sense of order and love of beauty in Your creation. Help me to honor Your judgment of Your creation. Observing the glory revealed in Your works, I stand amazed! You are a great God!"

PSALM 19:7

God's creation points me to Him, but it is in experiencing His teaching and instruction that I am changed. He knows how to make a perfect heart and wholeness of spirit. What a wonder God is!

"Lord, You are wise and good. In You I trust. Thank You for knowing just the right ways to reach out and touch my life so I can learn from You."

PSALM 19:8

The Lord knows not only how to lead us to conversion and instruct us, but He also knows how to disciple us by teaching us His principles. In addition, He knows how to reveal things to us that enlightens us. Loving God is never a stagnant relationship, but always growing and developing.

"Thank You, Lord, for disciplining us. Your principles are standards which have stood the test of time. They are life and have great value to me. Thank You for being such an incredibly wise God."

PSALM 19:9

Our fear of the Lord is clean and eternal. We may falter and fail along the way. But when God corrects us with His judgments, we discover His righteousness.

"Lord, I am truly amazed by the discovery of who You are through a variety of experiences. You are so creative and wise! I love how You show me Your great love in practical ways!"

PSALM 19:7-10
MATTHEW 13:44-46

The kingdom of heaven is here and now in our hearts if we give up self-centeredness and gain Christ-centered lives. It's a rare treasure to learn, know, and experience the truth of God's principles and standards.

"Lord, Your words, ways and wisdom are invaluable to me. I love the way Your principles stand eternally strong and pure. You are the REAL Joy-Giver!"

PSALM 19:7-11

I used a variety of ways, to teach, train and touch our children's lives to instill strong character in them. Sometimes we played games or read books. At other times I talked with them and shared experiences. Sometimes I had to demonstrate "tough-love" and give instruction and discipline.

Now think about—our Father. He loves His children more than any earthly parent could love her child and He uses a variety of ways to relate to us and instruct us. As we learn to listen, trust, and obey Him, we discover the great blessings He wants to bestow on us.

"Lord, how grateful I am that You are worthy of trust and are faithful to correct or bless me in the way that is best for me. There's so much security in knowing and worshipping You!"

PSALM 19:12-14

We have a strong tendency to take unfair advantage of someone's good nature—or of a situation. How often do we excuse our actions by saying, "Oh well, God loves me and He will forgive me anyway"? How rude and presumptuous can we get! If that kind of thinking governs our lives, we have missed the mark in understanding what true worship is!

"Let the words of my mouth and the meditations of my heart be acceptable in Your sight, O Lord, my strength and redeemer. Amen"

In Praise of the Righteous Judge

PSALM 9:1-4

Notice the determination to honor God in word and attitude. "I will…" is a decision and a commitment to act. Sometimes we struggle with choices before finally arriving at a decision. Then we struggle to live it out, and in the integrity to follow through.

In which of these areas do you battle? Reaching a decision, making a commitment, or following through?

"Lord, thank You for judging in righteousness. Keep me aware of Your righteousness so I can make wise decisions, strong commitments and follow through with them. I want to honor Your righteousness by rightly responding to You!"

PSALM 9:5-8

Don't you love the fact that the Lord will judge the world with righteousness and equity? Besides that, He, the Eternal One, has prepared and established His throne for righteous judgment.

"Thank You, Lord, for Your eternal, righteous judgment. I feel safe with You, knowing You are prepared to administer judgment with wisdom, love, uprightness and equity. It makes me want to rightly respond to You! I'd rather be a joy to You than a heartache."

PSALM 9:9-12

The Righteous Judge is One who is a safe haven for those who trust Him.

That's the difference between God's righteousness and man's legal system. Man-made legal systems have been known to convict innocent people. Sometimes a criminal is acquitted because he has a shrewd lawyer. But because God is a righteous judge we can have a securely abiding relationship with Him and a confident trust in Him.

"Thank You, Lord, for being my righteous judge, giving me perspective and wise judgment. Thank You for protecting and guarding me from destruction. You are too wonderful for words!"

PSALM 9:16

The judgments of God reveal His righteous and holy character. Think about it. God's judgments display His wisdom, mercy, and integrity. Our decisions, or judgments, reveal whether we have good or bad character.

I am not known for making good spatial judgments, so I have been known to walk off porches or into doors.

Today, stop and think about the things you do that require choices and decisions. What do your judgments reveal about you?

"Thank You, Lord, that Your character is revealed in Your judgments. That knowledge produces songs of praise!"

PSALM 7:8-10
GALATIANS 6:7-8

God's judgments are based on His knowledge of our hearts. We can't fool God. When we see or know Christians who don't act honorably, we should understand that it is not a real reflection on God—but on that person's lack of integrity. We must trust that the Righteous Judge can wisely deal with them. Remember God's correction is to teach and train. Our responsibility is to respond to Him—and not be the judge. Unfortunately, we don't know how to judge in righteousness.

"Thank You, Lord, that You are the Righteous Judge. Remind me that I don't have any business trying to judge others. I am to judge only myself, making sure that I am wisely responding to You."

PSALM 7:11

Rest assured that God is a righteous, just judge. Why do we worry about things and people out of our control? Turn to and trust our God, the Righteous Judge.

"Thank You, Lord, that You cannot tolerate evil. Thank You for being a just, righteous judge who teaches me good from evil, and godly principles on which to base life's choices so I can live a life that honors and glorifies You!"

PSALM 67

We all need to build a strong personal relationship with God to learn more of who He is. Then we are to share the truths about that wonderful relationship with others so they can learn the joy of knowing God.

Additionally, we all need to discover the value of righteousness. As we do, our ability to praise God will increase because, in close relationship with Him, we will have gained a better understanding of His standards.

"O Lord, teach me to have a better understanding of Your righteousness and Your standards, so I can enjoy a richer fellowship with You in joy."

What Does the Righteous Judge Do About Sin?

ISAIAH 53:1-2

Sin separates us from the holy, righteous God. Almighty God, made Himself vulnerable in the form of His Son, Jesus, even though He knew some people wouldn't believe or accept Him. And even knowing this, God, the Father, allowed His Holy Son to experience the full gamut of human temptations and problems, ultimately to be rejected and crucified for every person. Amazing, isn't it!

"You amaze me, Lord, that even knowing the cost, You willingly gave Your Son for me. Your unconditionally, sacrificial love humbles me."

ISAIAH 53:3-4

Isaiah's picture of the Savior written in this prophecy is so accurate. Each of us should feel shame for the many times we have despised Jesus. How many times and ways have we rejected Him? Although He knew He would be rejected, the Righteous One chose to be the bearer of our griefs, weaknesses, and distress. What a righteous, holy, and loving God! Why do we reject His great, sacrificial love?

"Lord Jesus, thank You for bearing so much so I can receive the benefits!"

ISAIAH 53:5

For our sins—yours and mine—Jesus was beaten, bruised, and chastened. Those cruelties paid for our sins of wrong attitudes and actions. With that atoning sacrifice, Jesus substituted Himself for you and me. If we could totally appreciate the awesomeness of God's holiness, the horror of sinfulness, and the hopelessness of isolation from God brought on by sin, how could we fail to be humbled and overwhelmed by the incredible, boundless love of God?

"Thank You, Lord Jesus, for paying the price so I might experience "at-one-ment" with You and Father God."

ISAIAH 53:6
1 PETER 2:22-25

It's almost inconceivable that the almighty, sovereign God willingly became vulnerable to our rejection, paying the price for sin so we might be at peace with Him. Yet we humans want to do our own thing. Why are we so proud and ignorant?

"O Lord, it's beyond my understanding how You can love so unconditionally and completely! Thank You for Your precious gift."

ISAIAH 53:7-9
PHILIPPIANS 2:5-8

Jesus willingly gave His all for you and me. The physical, emotional, mental and spiritual anguish that Jesus went through to pay the price for our sins is greater than we can comprehend! If we get even a small paper cut, we complain vehemently. Yet Jesus never, ever complained.

"Jesus, thank You for not just willingly, but uncomplainingly, giving Your life for me! Willingly and lovingly. Wow! You are awesome and wonderful!"

ISAIAH 53:10-11
JOHN 10:18

Think about what Jesus willingly did. He died, not as a martyr, but as a victor over sin and death. We worship the Lamb of God who suffered and died willingly for our sins. And we worship the Victor who has redeemed us. Awesome!

"Thank You, Lord, for what You have done. I worship You in deep appreciation for all You have done and continue to do for me. You are amazing!"

ISAIAH 53:1-12
PHILIPPIANS 2:5-11

Here is a portrait of Jesus, our Savior. He is victorious in a situation that, from man's perspective, appeared hopeless. Because of His great love and mercy, the Righteous Judge personally made sure that the punishment price of sin was paid. What is your response to our precious Savior?

"Thank You, my Lord and my God. I give my life to You in deep appreciation for Your great love. I am humbled by so great a selfless love. You are more than wonderful!"

Jesus, Equal with Father God in Authority

JOHN 5:22-23
REVELATION 5:12-13

Jesus willingly died to pay the penalty for our sins, was buried, then rose again as the Victor. He ascended into heaven where He sits honored and exalted by God, the Father. If Almighty God honors Jesus so much, shouldn't we also recognize, respect and respond to this wondrous gift of Himself?

"Lord Jesus, You are worthy of praise! It's simply amazing that You, Who uncomplainingly, willingly, and joyfully paid the high price for my sin, have become the Judge. You are worthy to receive the power and the glory, my precious Lord and Savior."

JOHN 5:24, 3:16-21

When we were newly married, we moved into a place that, unbeknown to us, was infested with an unbelievable number of cockroaches. It was horrible. I vividly remember turning on the light at night and seeing a huge number of roaches scurrying in every direction. Each time I read John 3:19, I think of those wretched roaches. I don't want to be like them, do you? Believe, accept, and trust the One who has proven His love and mercy. That's not such a struggle, is it?

"Lord Jesus, I believe You are the Son of God Who came to earth as a man to pay the price for my sin and that You rose on the third day to become the Victor over sin and death. Your display of love dazzles me. Thank You!"

JOHN 5:25-27, 1:1-5, 9-13

Isn't it interesting how John refers to Jesus as the Word! Jesus, God's Word, in the flesh, speaks God's truths. He has the same authority as the Word of God. Because He was God in flesh, He understood our trials and tribulations. He also knew that we could not bear them and would sin. Therefore, He gave His life as the complete sacrificial payment for the penalty for those sins. He has the right to be the Righteous Judge.

"Lord Jesus, it is comforting to know that You, as Judge, understand humanity so well. But it is also a frightening to realize how easily we abuse Your grace and deny You as Lord. Forgive me, Lord, for those times and restore a right spirit within me."

JOHN 5:28-30
1 CORINTHIANS 3:11-15

Even Christians will stand before a judgment throne. The things we have done will be judged by fire. Things done from selfish motives will be destroyed, but things done to honor God will be like precious stones.

People who have rejected Christ will be judged in a different way. Because they refused to accept Jesus' gift of atonement, they will pay the price of eternal separation from Him.

"Lord Jesus, I know that You are a loving and merciful God and You don't condemn thoughtlessly. I trust Your judgment because Your character has been proven to be merciful, just and equitable. You are the only One I can totally trust."

HEBREWS 2:17-18

Jesus is not only the Righteous Judge, but He is also the ultimate High Priest who ministers to people. He understands our inabilities and is ready to enable us. If we know Him as the High Priest who ministers to our spiritual, emotional, mental, and physical needs, we have no reason to fear the Righteous Judge.

"Lord Jesus, there are so many ways to describe You—Righteous Judge, Lamb of God, High Priest, the Word—to name a few. You always meet us at the exact area of need. Wow, I love that about You!"

HEBREWS 4:14-16, 10:22-23

Faith in Jesus gives us the freedom to go boldly before His throne of grace to receive mercy. Yet we can draw near in full, calm assurance because Jesus has opened the door and His loving arms to receive everyone who believes.

"Lord Jesus, You are the only source of true peace and joy. Thank You for all You have done to make it possible for me to draw near in full assurance."

1 PETER 1:3-9

God's power is revealed by our faith! He values our faith. We may go through times of testing, but that's to keep us strong. Each test of faith makes us stronger because we can discover the power of God through it. We may feel stressed by various tests, but He places our feet in a broad place. He is our High Tower and refuge. He provides all we need to pass the test. Our responsibility is to have faith, then trust and obey God's principles and direction.

"Thank You, Lord, for enabling me to deal with any crisis. I know You will provide me with all I need if I will simply reach out in faith and trust You. Thank You for taking me by the hand to lead me through the pitfalls of life."

Who Teaches Like Him
(Job 36:22)

ISAIAH 40:12-31

God is greater than any situation (past, present, or future), every problem or any difficulty. God is greater than every burden, every fear, and every concern. He teaches us through every circumstance, enabling us to be victorious over the challenges before us. Our responsibility is to hope in and look expectantly for the Lord.

"Thank You, Lord, for being there for me, teaching, comforting, and enabling me. Your grace is immeasurable. Thank You for the things in the past which Your grace heals, for the victory You give each day, and for the future that You know and wisely prepare me to stand strong in You."

ISAIAH 28:9-10

Whential someone is trying to teach us, we have two choices—be teachable or be unteachable. Our age, our aptitude for the subject, or even our overall learning ability is not as important as our having a teachable spirit.

A wise teacher creates an atmosphere that challenges and encourages. But it's up to the student to receive instruction and blossom with knowledge. God personalizes His methods to teach us a little at a time, giving us exactly the responsibilities we are capable of handling. But it's up to the student to receive instruction and blossom with knowledge.

"Lord, forgive my stubborn resistance to learning. I want my heart and mind to be openly receptive to Your creative ways of teaching me. You are wonderful in counsel, excellent in wisdom and work in me effectively. Thank You, my Lord! "

PSALM 32:8-9

In the first part of the Psalm David is crying out to God. These verses tell us God's response to David.

Years ago I faced almost two years of constant illnesses. The physical problems took a toll on me mentally and emotionally, and challenged me spiritually. Many times I cried out to God in anguish.

I can remember sitting in the hospital and reading these two verses, feeling as if they were words from God directly to me. I'm afraid that too many times I needed that bit and bridle to keep me focused. Horrible as that time was, I learned that the Lord is my hiding place as well as my loving teacher. It was an invaluable time of being comforted—and intensive learning.

"Thank You, Lord, for the tough times that teach us the truth, piece by piece, and the reality of who You are. You are my teacher and my hiding place, preserving me from destructive thoughts. Thank You for Your instruction that surrounds me with truths that set me free. You are amazing!"

ISAIAH 48:17

The Lord, our Redeemer, the Holy One, teaches us to receive benefits in every circumstance. He turns potential defeats into victories by teaching us godly principles and truths as we seek Him and His ways.

"Lord, thank You for teaching me how to make every situation spiritually profitable. You are wise and holy. I'm so glad that You are my strength, my Redeemer, my Lord, and my God! You are wonderful!"

EXODUS 4:10-12
2 CORINTHIANS 12:9-10

Although Moses experienced God's power and authority first-hand, he was hesitant to believe God's promise to use him. On the other hand, Paul learned that victory was not dependent on his strength, but on giving his weakness to the Lord. The Lord's strength is what made Paul (and all believers) "more than conquerors" (Romans 8:37).

The Lord teaches through a variety of ways. One way is learning from others. Can we learn from Moses what not to do? Rather than doubt God, let's take God at His word that where He leads us, He will provide all we need to be strong. Can we learn from Paul that our weaknesses keep us wholly dependent on our strong, capable Lord?

"Thank You, Lord, for my weaknesses because they help me discover Your enabling strength. Thank You for teaching me to lean on You in all things!"

ISAIAH 2:3
JEREMIAH 33:3

All relationships are two-way streets. A teacher teaches, a student learns. Friends help one another. Husbands and wives give one another love, support, respect, and honor.

In the same way, we are the responders to everything the Lord does in our lives. We are not God's puppets, but beloved ones who choose to respond to Him. In these two passages, what is required is to "come" and "call." God always answers those who "seek and ask."

"Thank You, Lord, for consistently teaching me Your ways when I come to You and for answering when I call. Teach me, Lord, to fulfill my part of our relationship."

MICAH 4:2
JEREMIAH 29:11-14a

Come, let us go to the Lord! He knows us better than we know ourselves. Because He loves us, He has wonderful plans for our lives. Let's seek Him wholeheartedly. He will teach us His ways and show us the way to go!

"Thank You, Lord, for the invitation to come to You and for Your promise to answer and direct me. You are always loving and gracious. I appreciate You! Open my ears to be able to hear Your call to "come" so I may sit at Your feet to express my love by listening and learning."

For He Instructs—In Right Judgement God Teaches (Isa. 28:26)

PSALM 119:65-72

One of the ways God instructs us is through His Word. He gives His Word to teach us good judgment, wisdom, knowledge, and how to rightly discern between good and evil—even between good and excellent. Our responsibility is to have receptive and responsive hearts, loving His Word and obeying Him as He teaches.

"Lord, thank You for Your Word that instructs me by telling me about things You've done in the past, as well as Your prophetic Word that assures me for the future. Thank You for teaching me Your principles and showing me how to respond to You responsibly. You are an incredible teacher!"

PSALM 119:9-12

Hiding God's Word in our hearts is meditate on it, as well as to memorize it. Godly meditation is not emptying our minds, but filling them with God's Word, thinking about it and discovering personal applications. That's one of the best ways to prepare ourselves to respond to God in ways that honor Him.

"Thank You, Lord, for Your Word that is a treasure hidden in my heart teaching and changing me to become the person You have designed me to be. Engrave in my heart Your Godly principles so my life will honor and glorify You."

PSALM 119:25-32

God's Word revives and stimulates us. A good teacher knows how to capture and keep the students' interest.

One of our children's first grade teachers said that they studied dinosaurs in January because the excitement of being first-graders had worn off by then. The thrill and anticipation of Christmas was over. So the first-graders had lost their joy of school. But the study of dinosaurs recaptured their attention and renewed their interest for learning. God is even wiser in His teaching methods. His Word not only revives us, but also stimulates us.

"Lord, I'm so grateful for Your teaching me in ways that revive and stimulate my faith and responses. Thank You for listening patiently as I deal with things that perplex me, comforting me and wisely teaching me Your principles applicable to my situation."

PSALM 119:57-64

Seeing and experiencing God's mercy should engrave His principles in our hearts. All of us have sinned. He told us that all have fallen short of His glory (Romans 3:23). God eloquently expressed His mercy and love to us through Jesus, our Redeemer. We are not redeemed from our sinful state by being good enough, nor are we trying to reach a cold, unfeeling god. We have a merciful, loving God Who reaches out to each of us to draw us to Himself.

"Thank You, Lord, for teaching me Your love and mercy by the ways You reach out to me. You teach by word and deed. O Lord, the cry of my heart is that my words and deeds will reflect the Your glory."

PSALM 119:124-128

When I consider Godly teachers in my life, my mom stands out the most. She taught me everyday hints for cleaning, organizing, cooking, etc. She taught me, by example, how to laugh at my own foibles and to find humor in life. I gained a great understanding of daily life from Mom.

I learned much about the character of the Lord by seeing Him as a vital and active part of Mom's life. His Word, in spirit and deed, came from His handmaid, Dorothea Hulet, to me.

"Thank You for Mom. Thank You for her commitment to You, Lord. Thank You for teaching me Your truths through Mom's life. I'm grateful for Your people in my life who teach of You by word and deed."

PSALM 119:129-136

When God's Word comes into our hearts, it is like turning on a light of understanding and comprehension. I struggle to see the way to go when it's dark. (Sometimes it seems that I can't even find the stairs to the second floor in our home.) It's scary and I feel hesitant to move. But when the light comes on, the relief and assurance changes everything! The more we give opportunity to the Lord to teach us through His Word, the clearer the way becomes and we can walk confidently forward.

"Lord, thank You for the light of Your Word and for the life Your words give to my heart and spirit. You are wonderfully amazing. I'm so glad You are in my life. I can't imagine facing a moment apart from Your guiding presence. Thank You for Your love."

PSALM 119:125-131

God's Word always reaps positive treasure. A couple of years ago my husband asked me to bake some bread during his sermon so the people could smell the bread baking. Mouths started to water, taste buds salivated as Jerry talked of desire and hunger to know the Lord and His Word. After the bread was finished, he took one small piece, smelled it, and talked about it. Then he slowly popped it into his mouth, savoring it. All the people's eyes were glued to him...with mouths open, desiring a bite.... Then we passed out the bread to everyone. They couldn't get enough! It was a marvelous object lesson for desiring and enjoying God and His Word.

"Thank You, Lord, for Your words that are sweeter than honey. Thank You for giving understanding of Your truth through what I experience. You are a wonderful teacher, Lord!"

September 16

PSALM 119:124-128.

Have you ever noticed that the more you are with some people, the more you love and appreciate them? Or have you ever had a teacher you've had that opened your eyes in wonder and helped you to want to learn? When I was an M.K. (Missionary's Kid) in the Philippines, I had a teacher like that, Margaret Condon. She impacted my life in more ways than one—not just in scholastic things. But she helped me discover an ability to be creative in art. Margaret loved all things pertaining to ships with sails and the ocean. I've found that I gained an appreciation and love for those things, too. I've never, ever forgotten her and am so grateful for all she did for me. If one godly teacher could impact an 11-year-old so deeply, how much more can God teach us wisely? The words of God give us understanding and discernment and we comprehend more and more of His character. Margaret would spend hours with me teaching me how to embroider (as well as many other things) and while I learned with my fingers, she talked, listened and I learned. Time with her affected my entire life.

"Thank You, Lord, for Margaret, who taught me so much. The principle of spending time, creating, talking, listening, and just enjoying was imbedded in my heart. I want to use the times all during the day to just chat and listen to You, Lord. Enable those precious moments so I may learn more of You."

The Teachable Heart

PSALM 25:4-5

How do you find it easy to learn? I find that to *show me* only, I'm still befuddled, especially when it comes to mechanical things. I must be given hands-on *teaching* that *leads me* step-by-step. God is so good because if we keep our hearts tender before Him, eyes on Him, then He is able to reveal His ways, teach by hands-on leading. His voice is soft and we must keep our ears sharp, shutting out other distractions!

"Thank You, Lord, for teaching me by the method I need so I can learn. You are good to me! I want to keep in line with Your voice."

PSALM 25:8-15

The Lord's teaching is based on His goodness and uprightness. He uses mercy and truth to instruct us. Our part is to recognize our need. As we understand His holiness, we see our own sinfulness. To be humble, recognizing His majesty, authority and love keeps us "guidable", living a life of integrity before the Lord by being faithful to Him, responding in like to His faithfulness. Love and worship the Lord in thought and action, honoring Him in all that we say and do are all the pieces of the formula to have a teachable heart.

"Lord, You are worthy of trust. You are the perfect example of integrity. All my hopes are met in You. Thank You for the loving way You teach me and show me Your ways."

EXODUS 33:12-14

Moses, because he, first-hand and step-by-step, had begun to know the great I AM, he'd been taught through the experiences and difficulties, and had undergone a major attitude change since Exodus 4:10-12. Drawing close to the Lord is progressive. Each step of the way, as we perceive, recognize and comprehend who He is, our faith grows stronger, our relationship is more established—line upon live, precept upon precept (Isaiah 28:10). A warning...we lose our faith and relationship the same way, one compromise at a time, one step back at a time.

"Lord, thank You for the encouragement of seeing Moses' life of faith grow through daily experiences. Keep my heart and mind aware of little compromises that could slip through the cracks and compromise our precious relationship. Show me. Teach me. Lead me, my Lord and my God."

PSALM 86:11
MARK 9:23-24

"Lord, I believe, help my unbelief." "Unite my heart to fear Your name." Don't we all experience those areas that are weak in faith and unbelief? But crying out to the Lord that we realize that there are areas of struggle in our faith is not dishonoring to Him. He knows your heart better than you do! The insidious compromises that creep into our lives, robbing us of a strong and growing relationship, come from those very weak areas. Worship includes honoring and trusting God while giving Him your weaknesses—even when it is belief in Him.

"Lord, my cry to You is the same as David's choice… 'Teach me Your ways, O Lord. I will walk in Your truth. Unite my heart to fear Your name' so that I may glorify You in word and deed."

Psalm 143:8-10

What is the best way to proclaim your commitment? In the American Christian wedding ceremony, the bride and groom proclaim their commitment by saying, "I ____ take you ____ to be my lawfully wedded husband/wife...." Before that there is the couple's relationship of love and the desire to spend the rest of their lives together. Here, David declares, "You are my God!" That is the reason for the hunger to learn God's will.

"You are my Lord and my God. I'm hungry to know Your ways. Teach me how to stay in Your will. You are wonderful, my Lord. I yield my soul and heart to You. For You are trustworthy, loving and honorable."

PSALM 90:12

D oes time get away from you? All the good intentions you have get swallowed up in the tyranny of daily life. I struggle with how to order my minutes, hours, and days so as to be fruitful and still find rest. So the prayer to "teach us to number our days" so that we can learn wisdom about how to live makes sense, doesn't it!

"Lord, please order my days to bring honor and glory to You. Teach me to realize the value of each hour, when to stop and rest, and when to get things done. Show me how to wisely prioritize my time. Lead me daily for Your glory."

PSALM 91:14-16

Here is God's response to the quest to know Him and to be taught by Him. When we make Him our Lord, He responds with His declarations of love and commitment to us. Read these verses several times. Let His Word take root in your heart.

"Thank You, Lord, for reaching out in love to draw us unto Yourself. And thank You that as we respond to You, You generously and graciously commit Yourself to meet us at the point of our every need. Bless Your Holy Name."

A Father To The Fatherless

PSALM 68:4-6

On August 9, 2000, my earthly father went to be with the Lord. Many years ago when struggling with the human frailties of my father, I was crying out to the Lord from my hurting heart. And I discovered that God would meet my emotional needs for a father. That released the demand in my heart that my dad be perfect and released God to be my father and to perfect my heart. My daddy is gone; he was 91½ years young. We'd grown closer over the years and because I had discovered the reality of Father God, I didn't have to make the emotional demands my daddy couldn't meet. Yet I discovered how to more and more allow my "Abba" to meet my emotional needs. Now I'm truly without my father. Yet I am at peace because I know my "Abba" is here for me whenever, wherever—consistent and faithful.

"Thank You, Abba, for Your Father's heart that reaches out continually to everyone. I praise You for You are loving, caring and always meet the needs of my heart. You are precious to me, my wonderful Heavenly Father."

PSALM 145:1-3
PHILIPPIANS 4:4

*W*hile comforting my Mother, we tried to spend
family time together each morning in hearing
from God's Word and in prayer. So I thought
I'd share some of our special times with you.

Grief is not just for times of death, but also for the loss of anything we hold dear—the end of an era—like when children leave home, a move, change of schools, friends that move, a change of work, etc. But the one constant is the Lord who never changes. All of our family has felt the presence of the Lord. His grace, peace and joy have permeated our spirits and our days. Even the times of tears have been healing because the God of all comfort (2 Corinthians 1:3) has comforted us. Gratitude for the gracious, loving character of God should be a constant in our lives. If that is true, then no matter what the circumstances of life, we can daily praise and rejoice in the Lord.

"Thank You, Lord, for Your gracious presence in our lives
during the crisis times as well as everyday living. Your
love is amazing. I love You Lord and praise Your Holy
Name."

PSALM 145:4-7

During the last 2½ years of Dad's life, every time we talked he was praising God. It was like a refreshing breeze to listen to him praise the Lord. It encouraged and challenged me. I'm so grateful for those memories. When we praise the Lord it doesn't just act as an arrow pointing the way for others, but keeps our own perspective more in tune with heaven.

"Lord, You are the great, awesome God. Let the words of my mouth and the meditations of my heart, as well as my actions, be pleasing to You and give You praise."

PSALM 145:8-9

Each step of the way, from the time Dad went into the hospital on August 5, we experienced the Lord's tender mercies and His graciousness in everything from travel arrangements to people who helped with small and large details. The Lord's hand was so gently—always leading, providing and encouraging. The amazing thing is that He's always there for us. It's in times of crisis that we become more aware of the reality of His daily presence. But even when we don't feel it, His character of gracious love and mercy never changes. So we need to remember to express praise to Him for He is truly awesome!

"Lord, You are wonderful. Your grace touches lives daily in abundance. You are our wise counselor and compassionate Lord. I am grateful for Your goodness daily expressed to those who trust in You."

PSALM 145:10-13

It's wonderfully encouraging to realize our creative God uses all His creative ingenuity to solve life's situations! Isn't it a comfort to know that the Lord knows how to bail us out of our struggles in such a way that we can be blessed and amazed? Then we can freely express our praise to our awesome Lord.

"Thank You, Lord, for the way You orchestrated our lives during Daddy's graduation to heaven. Thank You for Your wisdom in the timing and for each person who was touched by seeing the reality of You during that time."

PSALM 145:14-16

My dad was our cheerleader. He was always expressing to my sister and me his pride in us and his love for us. Over the last year, he had called my sister's voice mail to tell her how precious she was. He would end the call more often than not with "amen" rather than "good-bye". Daddy was so pleased to have a 2nd generation missionary to Japan that he requested when he died that my husband and I not return to the USA. Amazing God knew how to satisfy the desire of every member of our family. He had laid on my husband's heart the urgency of returning to the USA for July and August. So the Lord had us where we needed to be—even though we didn't understand why ahead of time! The Lord knew!

"Thank You, Lord, for knowing how to satisfy yearnings we don't even know we will have. Thank You for Your guidance that is full of mercy. You continually bless Your kids! I'm so grateful to know You!"

PSALM 145:17-21

Amazingly, last summer the Lord placed two separate strong impressions on Jerry's & my hearts. One was that I felt I had to see Mom and Dad in March. Jerry didn't understand the logic but supported me in this. It was the last time I was with my Dad, but I didn't know it at the time. The Lord laid the summer trip on Jerry's heart. It didn't make sense to me but I supported his sense of God's direction. The Lord knew how to work in each of us to accomplish His purposes for not just us, but for other members of our family as well.

"Thank You, Lord, for teaching us how to listen and blessing us with Your tender touch. You are a great and awesome God!"

Without Shadow of Turning

PSALM 31:1-2
PHILIPPIANS 4:6

The foundation to prayer is faith. Paul, while in prison for his faith, told us to present our prayers and requests with thanksgiving to God.

Note that David had a shadow over his prayer, "Let me never be ashamed...." He didn't want his hope in the Lord disappointed. Yet Romans 5:5 says, "hope does not disappoint...." Human emotions or past indoctrination sometimes invade our prayers and thoughts to cast a shadow on our faith and hope. But our faith and hope is in God, Who never changes. There is not even a shadow of turning with Him. If we are praying with thanksgiving, doesn't that give victory over our shadowed areas of unbelief?

"Thank You, Lord, for being constant. Thank You for Your incredible love. You are my Rock of Refuge and a Fortress of Defense to save me. I am so grateful for Your consistency and faithfulness and trustworthiness."

PSALM 31:3-5

Our Lord is not just the standard by which truth, faithfulness and trustworthiness is measured. He *is* truth, faithfulness and trustworthiness! Therefore, with great confidence we can know that He is our source of security and that He will faithfully lead us with gentleness. He teaches us to persevere, trains us so we develop strength of character, and tells us over and over of His love and commitment to us.

Our family found the truth of this after Dad's graduation to heaven. Everyday, every step we sensed God's leading, teaching and training. Not only that, but in many different ways we felt His abiding love.

"Thank You, Lord, for Your unconditional love. And thank You that You love deeply and with commitment. You teach and train each of us to become all that we can be. You are not only a safe harbor, but an encourager to us to venture forth in faith and believe all things are possible with You."

PSALM 31:6-8
NEHEMIAH 8:10b

We are to be grateful to God for His mercy towards us in the past and His daily dose of abundant grace. Then, with joy, we can know that He will meet our needs in the future. He is our source of strength.

Maybe your past feels black, or even painful. Does that mean God's mercy wasn't there? No! It was there! Sometimes we just need to ask the Lord to reveal how His mercy was reaching out to us in the painful past. Then we can ask Him to heal the memories of past hurts so we can confidently face each day with the assurance of His grace.

"Thank You, Lord, for all my yesterdays when You reached out to me in mercy. Heal the pain from past hurt in such a way that there will always be compassion for others, so I will reach out by Your love to show Your kindness and patience towards them. Thank You for the grace for today that meets my every challenge and need. And thank You for Your faithfulness for all my tomorrows. For You are my rock, my fortress and my strength."

PSALM 31:9-13
MARK 9:23-24

David says his strength failed because of his iniquity. Iniquity is the sin that we commit in our thoughts lives and attitudes—those inner things that no one knows about, but eat and erodes our faith. Those are shadow thoughts that creep in like weeds and threaten to overtake. What can we do to prevent oppressive and depressive thoughts that influence our attitude and then our actions? Paul says, in 2 Corinthians 10:5 that we must bring every thought into captivity that threatens our life of faith. Recognize the source of these thoughts—the enemy of our souls who is the father of lies. Then, with praise and thanksgiving, present our situation to the Lord. The enemy can't stand praise and will flee.

"Thank You, Lord, that You are greater and stronger than anything that would assault me, whether it is in my thought life or by others. Thank You for overcoming the shadows of unbelief that threaten. You are the victor and overcomer and I'm grateful for Your presence!"

278

PSALM 31:14-18

All of us have a sense of unworthiness at least some of the time. We feel that we must do something to "earn" God's love. The truth is, we are *all* unworthy. We are all sinners *SAVED BY GRACE*! It's not our worthiness, BUT <u>HIS</u>! He values us for who we are, not for what we do. What we do, when guided and enabled by the Lord, is our gift of faith and trust to Him. So the "truth of the service station" (the truth that keeps us going) is that God loves you.

"Thank You, Lord, for Your unconditional love which reaches out continuously. Thank You for Your infinite grace that keeps us going. Thank You for Your sacrifice so that I might be free. You are amazing!"

PSALM 31:19-22
ROMANS 8:31-39

O ur security is knowing God is by our side and we are more than conquerors through Him. He brings a sense of wholeness to our lives as His grace and love permeate our thoughts and memories, filling our hearts with love and giving us hope. He understands our pains and frustrations. He is always gracious and faithful to touch our hearts and spirits, providing everything we need to be victorious.

"Thank You for being the Victor over sin and pain. Thank You for being the God of all comfort. Thank You for making me whole. You are so good to me that I'm constantly amazed by Your gracious love."

PSALM 31:23-24
JUDE 24-25

God strengthens our hearts so we have strength of purpose, enabling us to withstand fears and difficulties. As we rely on God, He enables us to face any situation with the assurance that He is able to keep us safe and secure! Praise God!

"Thank You, Lord, for assurances in Your Word about Your loving care for each person. What a wonder and blessing it is to know You!"

The Lord's Loving Sacrifice

HEBREWS 10:13

The first sacrifice was made by God in the Garden of Eden to cover Adam and Eve (Genesis 3:21). Later in Exodus and Leviticus the Lord taught the Israelites about the Law and sacrificing animals. Why? Simply stated, it was for them to realize that people cannot live perfect lives and need a blood sacrifice to cover their sins.

"Thank You, Lord, for taking the time and effort to reach out and teach us Your righteous ways. It is too easy to think that we can do it ourselves and forget that our human efforts are weak and vain. Thank You for Your magnificent grace that reaches out, touching and changing lives."

HEBREWS 10:4-5
ISAIAH 64:6

Because the author was writing to people of Jewish faith, he uses the easily understood Old Testament examples of sacrifice, which make little or no sense in today's culture. So how does this apply to you and me today? How do we try to win God's favor or love? Do we stay busy doing "good" things? Do we try to "buy" God's love through giving? Is that what God asks? No! We are, by faith, first to accept Him, and then, also by faith, to follow His directions and express our gratitude by cheerfully and freely giving.

"Lord, thank You for loving me unconditionally. I want to respond to Your generosity of grace and love by having faith to trust and follow You each step of the way. You are my Lord and my God."

HEBREWS 10:5-10

S in. We experience it. We try to justify (make excuses for) ourselves or rationalize that it's okay because someone else does it. We try to sugarcoat our sin. But God doesn't sugarcoat anything. He tells us that impure motivations, attitudes, and our thought life is where sin starts—from the inside out. But just like God sacrificed animals to cover Adam and Eve and their sin, Jesus sacrificed Himself for our sin. We can't earn it, buy it, or bargain for it. But we <u>can</u> open our hearts and receive Jesus as our Lord and Savior from sin. We must turn towards Him and away from the failure of trying to make ourselves good enough.

"Thank You, Jesus, for paying the price for my sin by dying on the cross. Thank You for the victory You, and You alone, give because of Your resurrection. Thank You for loving so deeply that You gave up heaven to experience human life so we can know You understand our frailties. I'm awed and humbled by Your amazing love."

HEBREWS 10:11-14
PHILIPPIANS 1:6
JOHN 3:16-20

Big words like "righteousness" and "sanctification" can be overwhelming. Even if we do not know the definitions of these words, the "bottom line" is that Jesus paid the price for your and my sins. When we accept this truth by faith, He starts working in us to purify our hearts. His motive is love for us—not condemnation.

"You, who are perfect, laid down Your life <u>willingly</u> for my sins. For that, I am and will continue to be eternally grateful. I'm also so thankful that, although You have made me righteous by Your sacrifice, You continue to work in me to purify my heart and my mind. You are so-o-o-o good to me!"

HEBREWS 10:15-18

Salvation is a free gift. We don't earn it; we accept it. Why, oh why, do we complicate God's generous gift by trying to earn it? Acceptance by faith, that's it! Period! Paragraph!

When my parents first became Christians, they thought they had to dress a certain way and remove the "fun" from their lives to earn their salvation and show that they were "saved". More than twenty years later they discovered that salvation is truly a free gift and that we are set free to rejoice. If change is necessary, the Lord gently corrects us. It's up to us to willingly listen to His quiet voice and respond in obedience out of our love for Him.

"Thank You, Lord, for Your gentle voice of correction. Thank You for teaching that You give the grace so I can obey Your Word with a heart of love."

HEBREWS 10:19-22

Jesus sacrificed Himself. We must accept His precious gift of salvation. When we do that, we can draw near to God in unqualified assurance, absolute trust and confidence.

Our granddaughter, Kate, when she was 2½ years old, threw herself totally, freely, and enthusiastically into our arms. What a joy that is! Though she doesn't see us often, she knows we love her! That is the way our God wants us to come close to Him in relationship!

"Thank You, Lord, for welcoming me joyfully and lovingly, reaching to me with outstretched arms, embracing me. What a privilege and honor it is to be loved and welcomed so completely by You!"

HEBREWS 10:23-25

Realizing who Jesus is and what He's done for us is so precious. Clinging to Him releases our faith and trust, which, in turn, creates the "joy bubbles" in us that have to be shared. Fellowship with believers and worshiping together also encourages and stimulates our faith. It is incomprehensible that when people are struggling, they often decide not to attend church. That's the very place we need to be to support us during struggles, encourage our faith, and remind us to stay focused on Christ, not the problem.

"Thank You, Lord, for giving me fellow Christians who encourage and empathize. Thank You for the wonderful, loving people who are in our church. It's a joy celebrating You with them."

October 15

Triumph in Christ
ROMANS 15:5-6

Remembering that "we become like who we worship" and "nearness brings likeness," we need to zero in on verses that communicate the essence of who God is. What is the one thing we need when we are feeling impatient? Comfort! Wanting our own way and frustration with others (because they aren't doing things our way) are the basic causes of impatience. But our God, who is the source of patience and endurance, can and will comfort us. It's amazing how many times we have turned from God throughout history. How many times have you turned from Him? Yet, He is the eternal source of patience and comfort!

"Forgive my petty frustrations and times of impatience, oh Lord! I need Your patience each day and receive Your loving comfort. Let me see my life from Your perspective, oh Lord, my God."

2 CORINTHIANS 2:14

Don't you just love it*!* *"Now thanks be to God <u>who</u> <u>always</u> <u>leads</u> <u>us</u> <u>in</u> <u>triumph</u> in Christ"*. We all have problems and difficulties. That's a fact of life. *BUT*, by faith in Jesus, we will know and experience victory over the little—as well as the big—things! If you are not feeling triumphant right now, it's vital to remember to take your eyes off the situation and put your eyes on our triumphant God!

"Thank You, Lord, for being the Victor who leads us triumphantly. What a comfort it is to know that Your ways lead to victory over every situation and every challenge!"

ROMANS 15:13

Circumstances may not make us feel very triumphant. The process of learning comes *before* the experience of victory. Sometimes it just feels exhaustingly like defeat. But our ray of light is the truth that our God is the ***God of hope***. As we look to Him with our feelings of inadequacy and hopelessness, we can receive an infusion of joy and peace from this God of hope—the victor over death and sin. Eyes off situation, eyes on the focal point—our triumphant God. Then start feeling the joy bubbles and peace that overflow because your hope is met in God.

"Thank You for being the God of hope. I know You lead in triumph. I know You are the source of patience, comfort, joy and peace. I get into trouble when my eyes are off You and onto my problem— when I try to figure out a solution. Forgive me, Lord. I want my eyes to stay on You, for You are my only Hope!"

2 CORINTHIANS 1:3

Through life's challenges we, as believers, are given the opportunity to experience God's abundant mercy and comfort. Remember that everyone who is alive has problems of one kind or another. As believers, we have the opportunity to experience God's mercy and comfort!

"Thank You, Lord, that I can experience Your mercy and comfort! Open my eyes so I may see, really see, Your heart!"

2 CORINTHIANS 1:4

Problems and challenges are not accidents, but opportunities to experience God's mercies, comfort, and encouragement. The first step to victory is to view our circumstances as opportunities to experience more of God! Having done that, we can encourage others. The more we verbalize our "story," the more we recognize how good the Lord is!

"Thank You for Your comfort, Lord. Thank You for the ways You speak peace, joy, and encouragement to my heart and soul. Thank You for the people You send my way to give words and actions of comfort and encouragement. It's amazing! Satan's tactic is to make me feel alone in my struggles. But You, our victorious God, let me know that I am never alone!"

1 THESSALONIANS 5:23

The God of peace—when do we really appreciate peace? When there is upheaval, right? Peace is the "quiet" in the midst of trouble. Our God of peace is at work separating us from the things of this world that would pollute our spirit, soul, and body. God's peace at work in us, no matter what the circumstances, gives us the confidence to turn to Him more and more!

"Thank You, Lord, for Your amazing peace that draws me closer to You. Thank You for Your patience and mercy generously given to me. Thank You for the way You love so completely!"

1 THESSALONIANS 5:24
PHILIPPIANS 1:6

Each of us is "under construction." In Japan, at road construction sites, there are wonderful signs that, loosely translated, say, "Sorry for the troublesomeness of the construction. Your cooperation is greatly appreciated!" You have to love it! Our Heavenly Father is saying somewhat the same thing, "I know the work in you can be troublesome, but cooperate with me, and I will complete every good thing in you because I love you with an everlasting love."

"Lord, You have my cooperation. Thank You for the hope and confidence we have that You will faithfully complete Your good work. And thank You for Your grace that fills our hearts with comfort, peace and joy. You are wonderful!"

Secure In God's Everlasting Love

JEREMIAH 31:3

The concept of unconditional love simply boggles the human mind. Throw into that equation "everlasting love." It is impossible for us to grasp the reality of this incredible truth. James 1:17 tells us there is no variation or shadow of turning with the Father. Jesus Christ is the same yesterday, today and forever (Hebrews 13:8). The unchanging God loves you beyond measure or understanding.

"Thank You, Lord, for Your immeasurable, unconditional, and everlasting love. I can't comprehend it, Lord. I just accept it. Thank You for Your faithfulness and lovingkindness that never ceases, no matter what I do. I'm grateful. But more than that, I'm humbled by so great a love!"

TITUS 3:3-7

Have you ever considered (*really* thought about) how obstinate, thoughtless, self-centered, and deluded we are? Isn't it amazing how God, knowing us better than we do, loves so completely that He made provision for our sins to be forgiven so we could be made heirs to His kingdom? We cannot earn, nor do we merit, God's love. All we can do is respond to it and accept Him. It's so simple and yet so hard.

"Lord, I know I cannot work to earn Your love. It's just there, faithfully reaching out. All I can do is accept and choose to live daily with You as my Lord. My choice is to honor You by giving You my heart and my life."

2 THESSALONIANS 2:16-17

What incredible security recognizing God's love affords us! When our life is committed to Him and what we do is inspired and directed by Him, we discover His encouragement and comfort.

"Lord, every time I start to feel like what I do for You is inconsequential, You comfort me and encourage me through people or circumstances which renew my hope. I'm so glad 'works' don't earn Your love! It's so much more fulfilling to do things in response to faith in You. To know the security of Your grace fills me with hope. You are more than wonderful, O Lord, my God."

1 JOHN 3:1

The incredible quality of God's love is consistent in every area of our lives. It's inexplicable. We humans have a tendency to measure God's love by our finite understanding. God, knowing all of us have been hurt or wounded by others, allowed His Son, Jesus, to become vulnerable and become the victim of man's viciousness. Out of love, Jesus willingly laid down His life to pay for our sins, and victoriously rose from the dead so we could, in turn, live triumphantly. Not only that, but believers are called and counted as God's children!

"Thank You, Lord, for making Yourself vulnerable. It's amazing that You, the omnipotent God, have chosen to make Yourself vulnerable to fickle, undependable, self-centered man! Your love is absolutely INCREDIBLE! I'm so glad and grateful."

1 JOHN 4:7-8

Three simple words define the character of God—"God is love." We become like who we worship; nearness brings likeness. Therefore, it stands to reason that as we worship our loving God, His love will shine through us. Does anything tarnish the shine of God's love through you? We must each examine our hearts and find the reserved self-centered parts that haven't let the light of God's love and grace heal and make us whole.

"Lord, my heart is open for You to bring Your wholeness and healing. I desire Your love to shine through me. Reveal the self-centered areas so I can repent. Purify my heart. Lord, heal me. I need You. Thank You for Your love."

1 JOHN 4:9-11

The greatest demonstration of God's love is displayed in the life of Jesus, by His death that was the punishment for our sins and in His victory over death. Can we hear this too often? I don't think so! It's so easy to either take His life, death, or resurrection for granted, or to think of Him only as a great teacher. The knowledge of Who Jesus is and what He did keeps the reality of God's true, pure, and perfect love alive in our hearts and lives. Who is Jesus to you?

"Lord Jesus, I acknowledge that You are the risen Son of God who paid the price for my sin. You are my Savior. Be Lord of my life daily and in every way!"

ZEPHANIAH 3:17

Does this verse make you smile? Our Savior, who is with us, is mighty and yet rejoices over us with joy! He makes no mention of the past, nor does He recall it (Hebrews 10:17). God's love remembers to forget—we are not just saved, we are given a fresh start.

A favorite memory I have of my Dad is the silly songs he made up and sang to his grandkids. In my mind's eye, I can see him, rocking and cuddling the grandbabies and singing those delightful songs, telling them of his love. That makes it easy for me to picture the Lord singing songs of joy over each of His kids!

"Thank You, Lord, for remembering to forget! Thank You for Your might in the midst of us—for being Immanuel. You know what absolutely thrills me? Your singing and rejoicing! To me that expresses not just unconditional, everlasting love, but also the delight of loving. Thanks, Lord. You're great!"

Letting Go & Letting God Be God

EPHESIANS 2:1-3

Have you ever thrown meat bones or leftovers in the trash, then later notice a terrible smell coming from the area of the trash? Dead meat smells—that's a fact! Death and decay are yucky and smelly. Our lives before Christ are like that.

"Oh, no! Not mine" you may think. I've always been a good person.

However, we are all sinners. Sin is not measured by degrees or amount. Do you eat a piece of bread with a little mold on it? A little or a lot moldy is moldy! Realize apart from Jesus our hearts are smelly and yucky.

"Thank You, Lord, that believing in You brings new life. Thank You for resurrection power that brings light, freedom, and joy. You are wonderful!"

EPHESIANS 2:4-5

Why would God consider us? We not only throw out, but also get far away from dead, decaying things. But merciful God, in order to satisfy His intense and great love for us, has given us new life through faith in Jesus! Isn't it wonderful!

"Thank You for Your incredible mercy and intense love! Thank You for Your resurrection power that gives victory over sin. Thank You for letting me hear the good news about You and get to know You personally!"

EPHESIANS 2:6-7

Don't you just love the song, "Amazing Grace"? Think of the words: "Amazing grace, how sweet the sound, that saved a wretch like me. I once was lost but now I'm found. Was blind but now I see." Not only does God save us but He also gives heavenly perspective for our daily lives! Throughout history we can see this truth in Christians' lives. Who are some of the Christians who have influenced you? Why? Because of their perfect lives? More likely, it's because of the difficulties they overcame by God's amazing grace!

"Lord, thank You for the confidence of knowing that You will meet every need and show me the way. Thank You for people like John Newton, who wrote of Your amazing grace; for Corrie ten Boom, who learned to face the horrors of Nazi concentration camps by Your amazing grace; for all the people who have influenced my life because in their circumstances Your amazing grace was a brilliant light pointing to You, our loving Lord."

EPHESIANS 2:8-10

We can't earn anything from God by personal merit. It would, in some ways, seem easier to appease God with "good behavior". But that's not what He wants! What does He want? He wants our childlike faith and trust to believe in Jesus as our Savior and Lord. It's easy—right? Except that each one of us clutches to some "safeguard" so we will have a little control. But faith and trust means letting go of control and let God be God!

"Lord, thank You for doing all so I can relax in faith. Show me the areas of my life that I keep to 'maintain control,' so I can repent and release those areas into Your capable hands. I want to truly experience You in every area of my life."

EPHESIANS 2:11-14

O ver and over in Ephesians we read the phrase, "in Christ." The Greek word for "Christ" means the "Anointed One." Jesus was God's Anointed One to be the Savior of the world. When we believe in Jesus and accept Him as our Lord and Savior, the "in Christ" becomes reality. Because of our faith relationship with Jesus, we are in a fixed position of security and opportunity to enjoy the reality of God in our hearts, souls, spirits and lives.

"Thank You Jesus for Your life. Thank You for being my living peace and for breaking down the barriers. You are the only true bond of unity and harmony between God and man, as well as between people of different cultures and races. You are the one and only source of true peace! Thank You, Lord!"

EPHESIANS 2:14-18

Jesus is our mediator. He has paved the way! Many roads in Japan are twisting, turning, with 2-way traffic but not wide enough for two cars. So one stops and lets the others pass.

Several years ago we were driving to a meeting where Jerry was speaking. The roads were crowded, and it was obvious we weren't going to reach our destination on time. So we drove to a train station where he could board a train to get to his destination on time. What's the point of this story? Our lives get bogged down in twists and turns with congestion of worry and frustrations. But we have access to the One who is the way, the truth and the life—Jesus. He not only paves the way, but also intercedes on our behalf. He is our peace!

"Thank You, Jesus, for giving Your life for me. You are indeed, my peace. Bless Your Holy Name!"

EPHESIANS 2:19-22

The church is not just a building! It's people. In the truest sense, it is all the believers throughout history. The one constant in history and across cultures is Jesus, the Chief Cornerstone. He is the Solid Rock on which our faith grows!

"Thank You, Jesus, for being the Solid Rock for my life, our local church, and the church around the world. It's amazing to see how You work in us individually to bring us all together in unity and harmony."

Like a Shepherd, the Lord Provides

PSALM 23:1

Sheep, by nature, are helpless and dependent on their shepherd to lead, guide, and provide. A good shepherd knows how to care for the flock with T.L.C. (tender loving care). Most of us in today's world have never seen a shepherd at work. We can only really contemplate the entire concept.

I'm no authority on shepherds, but I know what it feels like to be helpless and need guidance. For example, I get a helpless feeling when the computer develops a mind of its own and I don't know what to do? Or, as often is the case, I'm stuck in a situation where culturally or linguistically I'm at a loss. We can all imagine the various scenarios in our lives when we need "hands-on" guidance. That understanding helps us cherish the treasure of the Shepherd's provision.

"Thank You, Lord, for being my Shepherd. I need You every day to provide Your godly wisdom for the circumstances of my life. I need You for the small, seemingly insignificant, things as well as the big tasks. I love the way You invest Yourself into every area of my life so I have the security of knowing You are always here for me! You are wonderful, my precious Shepherd! I really appreciate You!"

MARK 6:34-44

Jesus compassionately provided for people's spiritual, emotional, and physical needs. What does it mean, "moved with compassion"? Compassion is from Latin. The "com" means "with, together, jointly." The second part comes from "*pati*" which means "to bear, to suffer." Jesus saw the people and it broke His heart. He was moved with selfless tenderness directed toward their needs. His deep desire was because He understood every aspect of each person and was committed to alleviating their suffering. That's our Shepherd! Hebrews 13:8 says, "Jesus Christ, the same yesterday, today and tomorrow." Remember that Jesus knows and understands you, and He's committed to you, moved by compassion to care for you.

"Lord Jesus, all I can say is 'awesome'! Thank You for Your heart which is motivated and moved by love and compassion. I can relax in Your care. You're wonderful!"

JOHN 10:1-5

The shepherd knows who are His sheep. He even knows them by name. The sheep know the shepherd by His voice. That means that the shepherd talks to his sheep. David, as a shepherd boy, sang to the sheep in his care. Remember Zephaniah 3:17? We can know our Shepherd's voice. Our responsibility is to learn to listen daily. When we learn to listen, then in times of crisis or indecision, we will be able to filter out the other voices and concentrate on our Master's voice so we will know what to do and where to go!

"Thank You, Lord, my Shepherd, for daily reaching out to speak, sing, and touch me so I will be accustomed to Your voice and know what, where, when, and how You want me to be, as well as to move. It gives a quiet, calm assurance to know You are my Shepherd."

JOHN 10:9-11, 18

Jesus gave His life willingly...not just in His death on the cross, but He also gave up His rights as God (Philippians 2:5-8) to come to earth as a human, accepting all the weaknesses of a human body. He gave up heaven to become like you and me. Moved by love and compassion, Jesus willingly did all He could possibly do to reach out to mankind. What does that mean to us? We can have abundant life! That's for now—a life overflowing with the goodness of God, His peace, joy, love, and all that He is pouring into our lives! Jesus gave Himself wholeheartedly for us. Are we wholeheartedly accepting and responding to Him?

"Thank You for giving Your all so that I can be blessed beyond measure. I want my ears, heart, and soul to be tuned into You so I can truly experience Your abundant life. Together—You and I—today and tomorrow and forever! Thank You! I love You, Lord!"

JOHN 10:14-15

A good shepherd is courageous and faithful. He leads, protects, nurses wounds, nurtures, and communicates night and day. Think about what that means: the good shepherd *expresses* his love and commitment. Think about how Jesus wants to be your Shepherd. In what ways are you experiencing His love and compassion? In what ways are you blocking them? Why do you block it? Don't let any thief—spiritual, cultural, or other—keep you from fully experiencing the abundant life our Good Shepherd offers!

"Lord, show me the roadblocks in my life that keep me from fully experiencing Your abundant life. I am overwhelmed and humbled with all You offer and freely give. You are truly the Good Shepherd!"

PSALM 78:70-72

Although this Psalm is talking about David's shepherding skills, it expresses the heart of a good shepherd. The heart of a good shepherd is one of integrity. Integrity is more than honesty or correctness. It is an uncompromising heart. There is no deception, no artificiality, no shallowness, but, rather, a complete commitment. This is the heart of our Good Shepherd—integrity, compassion, and love. There is no spot or blemish in the character of our Shepherd.

"Thank You, Lord, for Your heart of compassion, love, and integrity. I appreciate Your skillful guidance, knowing it's based on the best possible motivations. You are awesome!"

ISAIAH 40:11-14

God's glory is revealed in His compassionate shepherding. Furthermore, God is much greater and more powerful than anything we face. God, who has unlimited resources, authority, knowledge, and power has chosen to limit Himself to be accepted or rejected by finite man. His love, compassion, and integrity will not allow Him to manipulate us or make us puppets. The choice is up to each person. Have you chosen to accept Him as your Lord and Shepherd? If so, are you allowing Him to lead or are you still trying to do it yourself?

"Thank You, Lord, for revealing Yourself to us. Thank You, Almighty God, for making Yourself vulnerable to my acceptance. My choice is You. I love Your compassion, Your integrity, and Your amazing love! How can I do anything but respond to You wholeheartedly?"

Like a Shepherd, the Lord Guides to Green Pastures

PSALM 23:2

Jesus is not a hired Shepherd just doing His job with one eye on the clock, the other on His paycheck. No. Jesus leads us with a pure heart of love and compassion. He makes sure we have spiritual rest and refreshment as well as challenges. The times of rest and refreshment restore and nourish us. The challenges purify our faith and motivation. Our Wise Shepherd knows what we need and when we need it.

"Thank You, Lord Jesus, for being a loving, compassionate Shepherd. You are so good to me! I'm grateful daily for Your care. Teach me to be what You want me to be. Guide me where You want me to go. Lead me to where I need to be when Your need me to be there."

1 CHRONICLES 4:39-40
PSALM 18:28-36

Shepherds traveled far and wide to seek rich, good pastures until they found the right place. Have you ever wonder what the sheep would be thinking during the journey? "What's taking so long?" "I don't like the pain of the trip!" "I just want to forget this and stop here!" But once they reached the pasture, they must have thought, "It's worth it!" The Lord leads to the best places, protecting, challenging, equipping us to handle crises, never giving up on us as He shows the way. We need to stop looking down at our circumstances and start looking up at the Shepherd who leads us.

"Faithful Shepherd, You do indeed lead me to the best pastures. Your way is perfect."

ISAIAH 58:11
PSALM 37:3-6

As we commit ourselves to Jesus Christ, trusting Him and learn to delight ourselves in Him, we will grow closer to Him. These are the ways our ears stay tuned to His voice and our hearts stay tender. Then our Lord is able to guide us through life's circumstances. He will not force us, even though He's omnipotent. It's always our choice to be led.

"Thank You, Lord, for being wise enough to allow me to make the choice. It's wonderful to know I'm not a puppet or a robot, but me—flesh and blood, failings and strengths. I am willing give my whole self to You because You loved me enough to give all that You are for me."

HEBREWS 13:20-21
PHILIPPIANS 1:6

Our wonderful Shepherd's guidance takes us to places designed to change us into His image and equip us to do His will. Difficulties smooth off rough edges, and reveal areas in our lives that we need to release to Him. As we let go of selfish, self-centered, and other-people-controlled areas of our lives, the Lord fills us with more love and power, showing us how to be more established in Him.

"Thank You, Lord, for never giving up and for always working in my heart and mind to establish godly, loving, gracious responses in me. My faith in You grows stronger through each "sharpening" experience. The hope I have in You strengthens my mind. You are a wonderful Shepherd!"

PSALM 95:1-7

A life of faith isn't achieved by digging in our fingernails and "hanging on for dear life." Enjoying a life committed to God by faith is based on appreciating the greatness of God. Our creative God will show us the way to go. Our hearts need to be tender before Him, responding in worship for Who He is. We must respond to His love by obedience—doing and being all that we know to do and be. The way we live our lives is a testimony to our God and an expression of our commitment to Him. What do others learn about the Lord by looking at your life? Are they repelled or attracted to Him?

"Lord, You are a great and wonderful God. I want my life to show the joy of knowing You. The opposite of a worshipping heart is a hard heart. My desire is to have a tender heart towards You so that my life will be an example of Your amazing love, joy and peace."

PSALM 100
PHILIPPIANS 4:4-6

Gladness, thanksgiving, and rejoicing are marks of a Christian life. If that is not so, then we need to examine why. It always comes back to the issue of focus, doesn't it? Is your focus on the situation or on our loving Lord? Does this mean that Christians don't grieve, feel disappointment, sorrow, etc.? No! We are human, and those are human emotions. Even Jesus wept. But the mortar that holds our faith blocks together is based on worshipping with gladness. It's imperative that we realize God is "bigger than the boogie man" and our circumstances." That realization should make us rejoice and be glad.

"Thank You, Sovereign Lord, that You are greater than any situation and that I can trust You with who I am, where I am, and where I'm going. You are always faithful and take good care of me!"

322

PSALM 79:13
MATTHEW 5:13-16

A basic principle of the Christian life is to give thanks to Him and let our gratefulness be evident, not just to those around us, but also to people of all places and ages.

"Thank You, Lord, for Your wise guidance and tender-loving-care (TLC). Your mercy and goodness bless me daily. I'm touched and changed by Your love. You are worthy of all praise and honor, O Lord, my God."

The Lord Leads to Still Waters

GENESIS 29:2-3

One of a shepherd's responsibilities is to make sure the sheep are watered. In water-hungry places like Palestine, shepherds had to search long and hard for pure water. Water was protected from contamination by a large rock. The sheep could be refreshed by clean, pure water.

"Thank You, Lord, that You give me protected places to be refreshed and restored. You always know how to satisfy my heart's longings. I'm grateful that You are my loving shepherd."

PSALM 65:9-13

Our creative God makes the water that restores and refreshes. He can make streams in the desert. Are you in a desert right now searching for refreshment for your soul? Although water is also to cleanse and purify, refreshment is what restores the heart. What obstacles are standing in the way of the refreshment you need? God cannot bless willful stubbornness. Each one of us needs to be tender before Him. Give the Lord your fears and struggles and let the healing begin.

"Lord, I realize that often I am the one who stops Your blessings from coming. Lord, I want my heart tender before You so You, my Lord, can create in me a clean heart."

JOHN 4:10-14

In the Middle East not all sources of water are pure. When Jesus said "living water" it was a picture of a spring bubbling up with fresh, pure water. The Samaritan lady to whom Jesus was talking had needs she didn't recognize. She had tried to satisfy her spiritual hunger and thirst with physical things. Jesus taught, "blessed are those who hunger and thirst for righteousness, for they shall be filled" (Matthew 5:6).

"Lord, thank You for the 'living water.'
Thank You for knowing me and meeting me
at the point of my needs. Thank You for
refreshing my faith. You are the source of all
my hope, joy, and peace. You alone are
worthy of all praise."

ISAIAH 12:1-6

Joy is found in the saving grace of the Lord. Isaiah talks of the wells of salvation—deep, eternal, refreshing, and cleansing wells of living water available to all who accept the salvation of the Lord. Such joy is contagious and needs to be shared. His joy and peace of should be the hallmark of your life if you know the Lord. If it isn't, that's not God's fault. He is the giver of joy. The problem is in receiving and accepting His gift of salvation. Joy and peace are there for those who believe in Him.

"Holy and wonderful Lord, thank You for the incredible provisions salvation gives. Thank You for the joy and peace You fill my heart with as well as purifying me. You are the faithful and trustworthy God worthy of all praise and honor!"

JOHN 7:37-39
ISAIAH 44:3

J esus was talking to the people on the last day of the Feast of Tabernacles, which was a time to remember how God led them through the desert by Moses. One of the rituals of the feast was to pour out water to remind them of how God provided water in the desert. The Israelites' real problem was not lack of water, but unbelief and a desire to go back to the familiar bondage of Egypt.

Jesus spoke of the Holy Spirit and used a familiar cultural example to make a spiritual point—believe and you will experience personal refreshment so you can reach out and touch others. Jesus was preparing to leave earth and made this an object lesson of how the Holy Spirit would be there for everyone. The Holy Spirit comes into your heart bringing light, teaching, and enabling.

"Thank You, Lord, that You never leave nor forsake us. You always provide what we need. We just need to remember to turn to You in faith, believing, and You will provide for us— not just what we need but in such a way that it blesses others, too. You are always kind and generous. I'm grateful!"

JEREMIAH 17:7-8

O ur Shepherd, God, provides for every one of our needs. To appropriate that provision, we must place our faith and trust in Him and follow where He leads. We have nothing to fear when we choose to believe. That doesn't show weakness, but strength and courage to admit your need and rely on Him Who is completely trustworthy.

"Thank You, Lord, for honoring our faith according to Your riches in glory. You are so good to those who trust in You!"

LUKE 1:78-79

Jesus is the light from heaven. He brings not only light, but also guidance. Our loving Shepherd never leaves us, but provides what we need, when we need it. He knows when to have us wait and when to have us go forward. We can stifle His provision by being restless and not wanting to wait on Him. But He teaches us regardless of the condition of our lives—if we will just pay attention!

"Thank You for Your guidance through all things…all the time. You are always faithful!"

Our Shepherd God Who Restores

PSALM 23:3

Life brings stress even if you are a Christian. Life has disappointments, difficulties, and sorrows. But (and this is a big BUT) when you know the Lord, He restores and refreshes you. Faith in Him is not merely having good ideas or a philosophy; it's about a personal relationship with the Lord of Lords. He knows how to refresh us and bring restoration.

"Thank You, Lord, for not just encouraging, but also for the refreshing You always give to restore. You are so good to me. I'm awed and humbled by Your loving care."

EZEKIEL 34:11-16

God searches out those with a heart tender before Him. There is no boundary or limitation to His reaching those who realize their need. We need to keep our own heart tender before Him and then intercede for our loved ones and those with whom we come in contact. May all our hearts be tender and receptive to God!

"Lord, I want my heart to always be tender before You. O Lord for those loved ones and friends who have not yet given their hearts to You, I pray that You soften their hearts. Send people to minister Your love into their lives. Teach me how to intercede for each person as You seek them out. Thank You for being the true loving Shepherd."

MATTHEW 18:11-14

Jesus' mission is plainly stated in verse 11: He "came to seek and save that which was lost." I love the picture of Jesus as the shepherd, searching for and finding the lost and fallen sheep. One who has turned his back on Jesus is always a lost sheep. But a lost sheep is also one who is disheartened, discouraged, lonely, and exhausted. No matter where you are today, Jesus is reaching out to you in love to restore and refresh you. Open your ears to hear and your heart to be refreshed and restored.

"Thank You for understanding and lovingly seeking out all who are in need of refreshing and restoration. You are so tender and loving. I'm so glad You are my Lord and my Shepherd."

LUKE 15:3-6

Think about the incredible truth here. The holy, righteous Shepherd doesn't condemn, scold, yell at, or lay any kind of guilt trip on the lost sheep. *He rejoices!* When someone turns to Him, He carries them on His shoulders and rejoices! The joy of the Lord is your strength (Nehemiah 8:10). That's not just the inner joy He gives, but His joy in you that encourages and refreshes!

"Thank You, Lord, for not yelling and scolding when You find the lost ones, but for rejoicing. Truly, You bring healing for the weary. Your joy is contagious. You bless so abundantly. Thank You."

1 PETER 2:21-25

Our Shepherd paid a high price so we can be free. Jesus totally understands our circumstances. He gave His life so we could receive freedom in salvation as well as joy and peace. Amazingly, even in difficulties, as we choose to respond as Jesus did, we will be filled with His love and strength.

"Lord, help me to keep my eyes on You—in all circumstances. Let Your love, joy, peace, and mercy be seen in me. Thank You for suffering and giving Yourself for me. You are precious to me, Oh Lord, my God."

MATTHEW 3:13-17

Jesus, the Holy, Sinless One, so identifies with us that He patterned each step we should take. Baptism is the symbol of repentance and new life in Christ. Only with Jesus. It really pointed to His death and resurrection that gives us His righteousness and enables us to live a victorious life in Him—not because of anything we have done. We can't earn it—but we can receive it!

"Thank You for patterning the steps we need to take. And Lord, thank You that I don't have to earn Your favor or love. Your love is beyond my understanding. But I gladly receive it and respond to You!"

ISAIAH 61:10

Righteous is to conform to God's ethical and moral standards... impossible for us. Only one could do that... Jesus. And yet the holy, ethical, and morally upright Jesus graciously solved the problem. On the cross Jesus received the punishment for our unrighteousness so that we could receive His righteousness when we believe in Him. Quite a trade off! We trade our garbage and gunk for His righteousness just by faith in Jesus as our Lord and Savior.

"Thank You, Jesus, for taking my gunk and giving me Your precious salvation and righteousness. And not just once, but for always You accept my sorrows, frustrations, and other yuck. Then You give me Your grace, joy, peace, and fill me with Your love. You are awesome! Thanks for all that You are and all that You do!"

December 3

Our Savior Shepherd

PSALM 23:4

I t all boils down to trust... sometimes our Shepherd leads us through dark and difficult times. Will you commit yourself, not to fear or dread, but to trust Him?

"Thank You, Lord, for being trustworthy! I may not understand the circumstances, but I know whom I believe and am persuaded that You are able to keep me, protect me, lead me and teach me wisely."

PSALM 3:3-6

Usually at Christmas our focus is on the joy in celebrating the Savior's birth. So here we are three weeks before Christmas talking about the *"valley of the shadow of death"*. Why? Have you ever felt stressed out during the holidays? Stressed out, wiped out, and totaled? Why? We work ourselves into a frenzy to make for *"happy holidays"*! So it seems that we should be checking and double checking with the Lord as to the best priorities for the holidays...as well as for every day. He is our shield and protector through the difficult times. Just be sure you don't step outside His shield to try and go on a self-assumed direction. The idea of having a Shepherd who leads is to be smart enough to follow attentively.

"Lord, lead me. Keep me from presumptuously going in the wrong direction. I want to stay right on Your heels, following You, so I can experience You as my shield and protector."

JOHN 16:33

The peace and joy that we have in Jesus is not dependent on outward circumstances. Neither can our confidence depend on our circumstances. It must be anchored in our Shepherd!

"Thank You, Lord, for overcoming the world and all its accompanying pressures. My strength and courage comes from You, the Victor over death and sin!"

LUKE 12:22-34

Worry pulls apart emotionally, strangling our faith and placing our focus on the problem. Trust and worry cannot co-exist. We each one have to make a choice to trust or worry. When trust is the priority, seeking God and living a life based on heaven's culture of godly principles becomes more a part of who we are. Remember that Christianity is not a philosophy, rather a relationship between a loving God and you! So the principle of trusting is not just a good idea, but a personal investment of relationship with the Lord.

"Thank You, Lord, for personally investing in a relationship with me...for giving Your 'all' for me. The least I can do is to respond to Your love by seeking You, trusting You, and responding with love to You.

2 TIMOTHY 1:7-9

Fear is never from God. Whenever you are afraid, pessimistic, or feeling hopeless, look to the source. Does it have any connection to God? No! Faith is what pieces the fabric of our lives together. Hope is threaded through every layer. And trust is the foundation. Stand for God unashamedly, grabbing hold of God's grace. Let your life proclaim the joyful truth of knowing God!

"Thank You, Lord, that You give power, love and a sound mind to equip each person with the ability to proclaim the wonder of salvation and the joy of knowing You. Make my life a shining example of the joy of knowing You as Lord."

ROMANS 8:26-28

"Valley of the shadow of death" times are when you can't see any solution. You feel grief and sorrow because of feeling lost. But the truth is not based on feelings or emotions! The truth is that even when we are afraid, we turn to Him, lean on Him, and trust Him. His will and good purposes will be the end product!

"Lord, You are forever faithful to me. Thank You for Your care that touches my innermost parts. Thank You for making all things work together for good. You are so good to me! I praise Your name!"

HEBREWS 13:5-8, 15

Trusting God means not envying others. True trust grabs hold of His grace to face our circumstances. We are never alone. Jesus never changes. Circumstances teach us to let go of the things that keep us from living a life pleasing to the Lord. The sacrifice of praise... instead of grumbling and complaining when life is difficult, praise the unchanging, loving, caring God who is completely trustworthy.

"Thank You for never changing! When everything around me is changing, You are the one constant in my life. You are a wonderful Shepherd. I love You, Lord!"

The Shepherd Who Protects & Sustains

Psalm 23:5

Who are our enemies? Are our enemies the ones who criticize us, gossip about us, complain about us, nag us, etc.? It feels that way. But our greatest enemies are not the ones who sling the arrows. The enemies that win the most battles are the things inside us...like pride, self-centeredness, anger, envy, etc. Psalm 37:3 tells us to "trust in the Lord and do good, dwell in the land and feed on His faithfulness" *(NKJV).* We can't control our circumstances no matter how hard we try, but we can trust in the goodness of the Lord and respond from that perspective instead of reacting with our self-centered "nuclear reactor". We can dwell with our minds anchored in the knowledge of God's faithfulness and let that feed us emotionally and spiritually. The Lord has a feast ready for us in the middle of every crisis...when we stay focused on His character. Trust God's heart of love for you!

"Thank You for Your heart and character of love. Lord, I know that, no matter what the circumstances are, I can fully trust You to overflow my heart and emotions with Your grace to meet every situation."

PROVERBS 16:7
PSALM 37:23-29

It's so easy to fall into the trap of being a "men-pleaser"...living so that others will approve of you. The problem is that people are fickle and you just can't please them all the time! <u>But</u> if we choose to live a life committed to the Lord, we find peace, joy, love, and a contentment that defies description. The only One who matters in the overall scheme of things is the Lord. So we each need to evaluate and decide who we are trying to please...God or man.

"Thank You, Lord, for Your loving care. It's so good to know that a life lived in commitment to You is the only way we will find true peace. You are so good to those who trust in You. Help me, Lord, to stay focused on Your character, enabling me to make choices that please You."

PSALM 3

Don't you love the imagery of the Lord...our shield, the One who we can glory in, our encourager! Here, although surrounded by enemies, David says "I lay down and slept...for the Lord sustains me!" What is your perception of the Lord? Do you see Him as your shield and cheerleader? We must truly realize "if He be for us, who can be against us?" (Romans 8:31). Not only does He want to be a shield, but He also looks for ways to encourage us. He is our cheerleader. The shepherd role is just a part of who He is to us. He wants to meet us at the point of each of our emotional needs.

"Thank You Lord for loving so greatly, for protecting us when we turn to You, for being our cheerleader. Thank You for the peace only You can give in the midst of our circumstances and for sustaining us. You are awesome!"

LUKE 6:27-38

The Lord prepares a table for us in the presence of our enemies...those self-inflicted enemies can be defeated by God's grace. But what about the people behind the verbal and physical arrows? "For God so loved the world *(that's everybody!)* that He gave His only Son...". Jesus came not just for the "sweet and darling" people, but for the angry, bitter, backstabbers too! So of course we are to love our enemies in every possible way. Jesus patterned the lifestyle of love and forgiveness. When we believe the vindictive, manipulative words and actions of enemies and respond in love, the enemy loses. God wins! We win and have victory. It's a tough battle over our human desires to give like action back. But the victory of love is exhilarating and well worth the effort to stomp on our pride and anger. Remember that the Lord doesn't just sustain. He's our encourager as well!

"Lord, what You ask us to do to show love to those who wound with words and actions is excruciatingly hard. But I thank You for Your grace that enables and sustains me through all circumstances. Let Your love be the guiding force of my life!"

COLOSSIANS 3:12-17

Forgiveness is the secret to real victory and is the only way not to be controlled by the evil intents of man. Jesus' prayers pattern this both in Matthew 6:12-15 and Luke 23:34. If Jesus could forgive while hanging on the cross, can we not grab hold of His grace powered by resurrection power motivated by a heart of love and make the determined choice to forgive?

"Lord, teach me how to forgive as You do. I need Your love to flow through me to forgive others. Only Your love can give me the courage to let go of my hurts and forgive. Thank You for freely giving Your enabling love!"

PSALM 27

avid was a man who made wrong choices, compromising God's principles. And yet God calls him a man after His own heart. How can that be? He always recognized his sin as sin and turned in repentance to God. What has that to do with our Shepherd who protects and sustains? Notice verse 1 of Psalm 27. What is the Lord? Light and salvation! Our Shepherd God lights the way to lead us. He saves us from the sins that darkened our spirits and lives. We have nothing to fear for the Lord is, in truth and in deed, the strength of our lives.

"Lord, my cry is the same as David's, 'teach me Your way.' For You are my only hope! Thank You for the light You unselfishly give. You are the Rock upon which I want my life built."

PSALM 91

The security of trusting in the Lord is in verses 14-16, for this is God's response to the declaration of verses 1-13. Look at God's promises expressed in the "I wills". I will deliver. I will set him on high (give godly perspective). I will answer your call. I will be with him in trouble (Immanuel...God with us!). I will deliver and honor him. I will satisfy him and show My salvation. Just think on these wonderful promises! Focus on the Lord, commit your life, responses and situations to Him and discover the adventure of faith!

"Lord, You are the One I trust. I want to be where and what You call me to be, for You are my only source of life and light. You are precious to me, O Lord, my Strength and my Redeemer."

Our Shepherd Reaches Out with Goodness and Mercy

PSALM 23:6

God's eternal, unfailing love reaches out, surrounding and leading us in ways we don't comprehend. The power of love is an amazing thing. The Lord doesn't manipulate. He is not a "control freak." He gives us the choice to follow and to experience. In addition, the degree of commitment is individual. But He never stops calling our hearts and reaching out. How are you responding?

"Lord, it is humbling to realize that You, the Creator of life, allow Yourself to be vulnerable to the ones You designed and created. Such commitment to love unconditionally and unfailingly is beyond my comprehension. Thank You for Your love, goodness, mercy and grace. I am in awe of You."

Isaiah 7:14
Luke 1:26-38

Mary was an ordinary young woman, just doing everyday things when God called her to an extraordinary experience. We don't know whether she was highly educated or outwardly beautiful. But it wouldn't have mattered. God looked at her heart, not at her accomplishments. God saw that her heart was for open, vulnerable, and responsive. She couldn't comprehend the "how's," but she accepted the word she heard. The special key was that she believed the truth, "For with God, nothing is impossible." (Luke 1:37)

"Lord, my prayer is that my heart will be as open and responsive to You as Mary's. I believe You when You say, 'for nothing is impossible.''

LUKE 1:46-55

Mary gives us a beautiful example of how to worship in spirit and truth. Not only did she respond to God's call, she also put her life into His hands even though she knew, culturally, she was placing herself in the way of criticism and scorn. Still, she was able to respond with praise and see heaven's perspective. Her perspective made the difference in her response! May ours do likewise.

"Lord, my desire is to keep my eyes and heart focused on Your love, mercy and goodness so at every opportunity I will worship You in spirit and respond in action!"

ISAIAH 9:6
LUKE 2:7

Divinity, clothed in humanity, came. God's gift of love, Jesus, our Immanuel (God with us) was born in a humble stable because there was no room in the inn. Shocking!

But what about your heart? Are you too busy to prepare Him room to enter? Are your heart and mind cluttered with fears, bitterness, anger, etc. so they are closed to allowing Him to enter in and bring light and life?

"Lord Jesus, thank You for loving so deeply that You made Yourself vulnerable. Help me, Jesus, my Immanuel, to respond to You the same way...open and vulnerable. I want You to have all the rooms in my heart."

LUKE 2:8-20

Ordinary men doing a common job…but God proclaimed to them, through the angels, that the Christ had come for all peoples! The Lord, who is our Shepherd, revealed to shepherds. Their response to God's word was immediate, and these men's lives would never be the same again, for they had been touched and changed by recognizing Christ, the Lord, worshipping in spirit and responding in action.

"Jesus, it's hard to comprehend that You made Yourself vulnerable and came as a baby. There is no way to understand that kind of committed love reaching out to touch people. Thank You for loving that much!"

December 22

LUKE 4:18-21
(quoted from Isaiah 61:1-2)

Jesus was the fulfillment of this promise, given hundreds of years before He was born. But people didn't believe Jesus any more then than they do now.

How often have you thought, *if only I could see Jesus, then I could believe?* But faith is seeing God with the heart, not with the eyes. Nor is it an emotion. Many have seen God's miracles and responded emotionally to the experience, but still didn't open their heart to the adventure of faith. Some of the stumbling blocks to faith are pride, self-righteousness and fear of what others will say. How do you see God?

"Lord, You've said that we will see the reality of Your kingdom in our hearts when we recognize our need for You and mourn the fact that we are separated from You. Lord, keep me from presumptuous sins that turn my heart from You. I want my heart tender before You, hungering and thirsting for more or You!"

MATTHEW 2:1-12

Wealthy men of influence came seeking the Messiah. These were not Jewish people. They were Gentiles. Their hearts were seeking God because God had spoken to them in the way they understood *(Psalm 19:1-4)*. Others had the knowledge but not the heart to seek *(verses 4-5)*. These wealthy, influential, intelligent men fell down and worshipped the God Who had become a child. They gave their best gifts to Him as an act of worship. If you were one of the people in these verses, who would you be? The one trying to destroy what God is doing, the ones with head knowledge and no heart to seek or the ones allowing your intelligence to open your hearts to seek and give to Christ?

"I pray, Lord, that my heart will always seek You!"

Jesus, Pattern for Our Lifestyle

MICAH 5:2
LUKE 2:4-7

This promise was given some 700 years before Jesus' birth! Amazingly, a decree by a pagan ruler was God's way to fulfill prophecy.

Never be surprised by the unusual ways God chooses to bless us and work for us. The process wasn't very comfortable for Mary or Joseph, but the outcome blessed all people!

"Lord, I think You have a real sense of humor to perform the wonders You do by the methods You use. A life of faith with You is not boring! Thank You for coming as a baby, living a day-to-day life. Today we celebrate You, our Immanuel!"

MATTHEW 20:26-28
ROMANS 12:1-3

From a humble birth to a life of service…God in flesh gave of Himself. Love in action! As we give our lives to God, serving one another, following Jesus' pattern, we discover real victory as well as purpose and joy in living.

"Lord, thank You for being an example of true humility. Change me each day to become more like You."

JOHN 13:3-5

Humility is *not* "degrading yourself." Jesus knew who He was and what His capabilities were. He knew His purpose. He gave Himself, even to the one who would betray Him. Love enabled Jesus to be vulnerable to acceptance or rejection. It was the strength that enabled Him to give of Himself.

"Thank You for Your perfect love! Enable me to know the value You have placed on me so I can confidently serve others in Your name, showing Your unselfish, giving love. You are my strength!"

ISAIAH 53:5
ROMANS 5:6-8

Vulnerable love is giving, always giving. Love didn't—and still doesn't—demand us to be perfect before receiving Jesus as Lord and Savior. Jesus gave His life for <u>all</u> of us, because all of us miss the mark of God's perfection. The wonder is not that we make ourselves "good enough" for God (we can't). The wonder is God, Himself, makes us good through faith in Jesus. God places value on us. We are so valuable that God gave His best for our worst. What love!

"Thank You, Lord Jesus, for taking the penalty for all the wrongs I've done and will do…for giving Yourself completely for me. Thank You for Your perfect love given to imperfect me. Thank You for demonstrating what love is all about."

PSALM 109:4
LUKE 23:34

Forgiveness—complete and total forgiveness—is one of the hardest things we humans ever try to do. Jesus taught that total forgiveness includes forgetting. God forgives *and* forgets. Jesus, God who became man, forgave, while hanging on the cross. He forgave Peter for denying Him. He forgives you and me. Now, what is that petty issue we have trouble forgiving? For Jesus' sake, and in Jesus' name, forgive!

"Thank You, Lord, for not just forgiving, but also for forgetting forgiven sins. You are more than gracious. You are total, pure, and complete love!"

PHILIPPIANS 2:3-8
1 JOHN 1:9

We are approaching the end of a year. Resolutions are being made, and we are finalizing details in order to start the New Year fresh and clean. But what about our hearts? Shouldn't we be as fresh and pure as possible there, also? Let's let the same attitude of humble-mindedness that was in Christ Jesus be in us as well.

"Oh, Lord, show me how to have the same attitude as You did. Show me the areas of my life that need Your purification, then enable me by Your grace to yield those areas to You."

PHILIPPIANS 2:9-15

Jesus' sacrifice provided every benefit that heaven can give. When we give our all willingly, as He did, without grumbling or complaining, we are honoring the Lord for what He did for us. And in due time the Lord will reward our faithfulness.

"Lord, as I close out this year, I want to open up more to You. I want my life to honor You and express my love and appreciation for all that You are and all You have done for me."

Zephaniah 3:17

Our Savior and Lord does the most amazing things! He, the almighty One, Creator of the universe, the Sovereign God rejoices over you and I with joy! Imagine that! He doesn't beat us down with condemnation over our past sins. When we turn to Him in repentance and seek His face, He rejoices and in His great unconditional love he makes no mention of past sins. The amazing thing is that He, the all-knowing One, chooses to not even recall our past sins. They are forgiven and forgotten. The Almighty God rejoices and sings over us! Imagine that! A song of rejoicing! Wow! How wonderful it is to be in relationship with a God like that!

"Thank you, Lord, for rejoicing and singing over me! The only place where surrender brings total victory and joy is when we entrust our lives and cares into Your hands! You are amazing and awesome. I am so glad that You are my Lord and my God! You are truly mighty and I rejoice in knowing You."

A Final Word

It is our sincere desire that you have been blessed by these devotionals. Please take the time to write to us if anything in particular stood out for you or helped you through a uniquely difficult or victorious time. We'd love to hear from you.

Our permanent address in America is

Jerry & Robin Schroeder
Son-Risen Ministries
PO Box 700615
San Antonio, TX 78270

Additional copies of this book are available from the above address.

Our God in an awesome God!